The Laws of Nature

An Infallible Justice

His Divine Grace

A.C. Bhaktivedanta Swami Prabhupāda

Founder-*Ācārya* of the International Society for Krishna Consciousness

The Bhaktivedanta Book Trust

Readers interested in the subject matter of this book are invited by The Bhaktivedanta Book Trust to correspond with its secretary at the following address:

The Bhaktivedanta Book Trust
ISKCON Temple,
Hare Krishna Land,
Juhu, Mumbai 400 049, India.

The Bhaktivedanta Book Trust
PO box: 341445
Los Angeles, Califorinia,
United States of America 90034.

Website / E-mail :
www.indiabbt.com
admin@indiabbt.com (Within India)
bbt.usa@krishna.com (Outside India)

The Laws of Nature (English)

1st printing in India : 10,000 copies
2nd to 18th printings : 3,50,000 copies
19th printing, April 2014 : 75,000 copies

ISBN : 978-93-82716-40-2

Published and Printed by The Bhaktivedanta Book Trust.

DH4N

CONTENTS

INTRODUCTION

Man prides himself on being a creature of reason, above the lowly beasts. Yet it seems that when he applies his reason to unlocking the secrets of nature for his benefit, he sinks deeper and deeper into a quagmire of intractable problems. The internal combustion engine gets us where we're going faster, but also results in choking air pollution, the greenhouse effect, and a dangerous dependence on oil. Harnessing the atom gives us cheap energy, but also leads to weapons of mass destruction, Chernobyl, and a rising tide of dangerous radioactive waste. Modern agribusiness produces a dizzying variety and abundance of food at the supermarket, but also results in the death of the family farm, the pollution of ground water, the loss of precious topsoil, and many other problems.

It's clear we're missing something in our attempts to harness the laws of nature for our own purposes. What is that "something"? We find out in the very first mantra of the Īśopaniṣad, the foremost of ancient India's books of wisdom known as the Upaniṣads: "Everything in this creation is owned and controlled by the Lord. One should therefore accept only those things necessary for himself, which are set aside as his quota, and one should not accept other things, knowing well to whom they belong."

In nature we see this principle at work. Nature's arrangement, set up by the Lord, maintains the birds and beasts: the elephant eats his fifty kilos per day, the ant his few grains. If man doesn't interfere, the natural balance sustains all creatures.

Any agriculturalist will tell you the earth can produce enough food to feed ten times the present human population. Yet political intrigues and wars, unfair distribution of land, the production of cash crops like tobacco, tea, and coffee instead of food, and erosion due to misuse ensure that millions go hungry, even in wealthy countries like the United States.

We must understand the laws of nature from the viewpoint of the Supreme Lord, who has created these laws. In His eyes all the earth's inhabitants—whether creatures of the land, water, or air—are His sons and daughters. Yet we, the human inhabitants, the most advanced" of His creatures, treat these sons and daughters with great cruelty, from the practice of animal slaughter to destruction of the rain forests. Is it any wonder that we suffer an unending series of natural disasters, wars, epidemics, famines, and the like?

The source of our problem is the desire for sense gratification beyond the consideration of anyone else's rights. These rights are the rights of the child in relation to the father. Every child has the right to share the wealth of his father. So creating a brotherhood of all creatures on earth depends on understanding the universal fatherhood of God.

As we have seen, the Vedic literature declares that the Supreme Lord owns and controls the entire creation. Not a blade of grass moves without His sanction. He is the complete whole. Then what is our position? Again we find the answer in the Vedic literature: Our natural, constitutional role is to serve God. He is the supreme enjoyer, and we are meant to take part in His enjoyment through service to Him, not by trying to enjoy separately. He is omnipotent and thus completely independent. Our minute independence is a tiny reflection of His total independence. It is our misuse of that minute independence and our attempt to enjoy separate from Him that have resulted in our current predicament.

Why do we misuse our independence? Because we are ignorant of our real nature. The first lesson of the Vedic wisdom is that we are not bodies but rather spirit souls—minute particles of consciousness dwelling within the body and animating it. Just as a car is a machine that allows a driver to travel from point A to point B, the body is a machine that allows the spirit soul to act and to experience sensations and thoughts within the Lord's material nature. When we understand our true identity as spiritual beings, part and parcel of the Supreme Spirit, God, we understand that we are meant to serve Him just as the hand or foot serves the whole body.

Our problem, however, is that we forget our identity separate from the body and instead misidentify ourselves with it. If a person happens to be born in America he considers himself an American, if he is born in France he considers himself a Frenchman, and so on. We also identify ourselves according to our sex, race, creed, social status, etc. But all these qualities apply only to the body, not the soul. Therefore embracing them as our true identity causes us to forget the Lord and our relationship with Him, and to see ourselves as independent enjoyers of His material nature.

The Vedic literature explains that human activity, when devoid of service to the Lord, is governed by a subtle law known as the law of *karma*. This is the familiar law of action and reaction as it pertains to what we do in this world and the enjoyment or suffering we experience as a result. If I cause pain to another living being, then as surely as the wheel of life turns, I will be forced to suffer similar pain. And if I bring happiness to another, a like pleasure awaits me. At every second, with every breath, our activities in this material world cause enjoyment and suffering. To facilitate these endless actions and reactions, there has to be more than just one life. There has to be reincarnation.

Until recently the idea of reincarnation, while universally accepted in India and other Eastern countries, had found few adherents in the West. The Church banned the philosophy of reincarnation centuries ago. This is a long story dating as far back as the history of the early Christian Church between 300 A.D. and 600 A.D. Recounting this controversy is not within the scope of this book, but the denial of this important concept has left a void in the world view of the Western peoples.

However, in the last decade or so many thinkers in the West have begun to take the idea of reincarnation seriously. For example, Dr. Michael Sabom of Emory University Medical School has written a book entitled *Recollections of Death: A Medical Investigation* (1982), which details his studies confirming the out-of-body experiences reported by cardiac arrest patients. Sabom writes, “Could the mind which splits apart from the physical brain be, in essence, the soul, which continues to exist after the final bodily death, according to some religious doctrines?"

And Dr. Ian Stevenson, a psychiatrist at the University of Virginia, in his book *Twenty Cases Suggestive of Reincarnation* (1966), has documented and verified past-life memories in young children. Other studies using such methods as hypnotic regression indicate that the idea of reincarnation may soon gain acceptance among mainstream scientists in the West.

The Vedic literature makes reincarnation of the soul a central feature in its explanation of human destiny. And the logic is obvious when we consider a simple question like the following: Why is one child born to wealthy parents in the United States, while another is born to starving peasants in Ethiopia? Only the doctrine of *karma* and reincarnation—reward and punishment carried over many lifetimes—answers this question easily.

The Laws of Nature: An Infallible Justice has been compiled primarily from two sources. The first is a series of talks given on the *Śrī Īśopaniṣad* by His Divine Grace A.C. Bhaktivedanta Swami Prabhupāda (see "The Author," p. 84). Delivered in Los Angeles in the spring of 1970, these talks provide an illuminating account of how the universe really operates. The second source is Śrīla Prabhupāda's commentated translation of the *Śrīmad-Bhāgavatam*. From the Third Canto of this monumental work we here reproduce Chapter Thirty, titled "Description by Lord Kapila of Adverse Fruitive Activities." In this section we learn the fate of the sinful soul who transgresses the laws of God's nature and incurs punishment according to the law of *karma*.

In one of his *Īśopaniṣad* talks, Śrīla Prabhupāda says, "If you do good work, you will have so-called enjoyment in your next life—but you will remain bound up in the cycle of birth and death. And if you do bad work, then you will have to suffer the sinful reactions and also remain bound up in birth and death. But if you work for Kṛṣṇa, there are no such reactions, good or bad, and at the time of death you will return to Kṛṣṇa. This is the only way to break the bonds of *karma*."

And this is the only way for society as a whole to mitigate the sufferings mentioned earlier. While we are in this world there is no getting rid of suffering all-together, for, as the Vedic teachings recognize, this material world is by nature a place of suffering. Ultimately we are powerless in the midst of a vast array of natural forces. The hope, therefore, is to know and follow the will of the Supreme Lord, the master of nature. Only in this way can we transcend the laws of nature, end the cycle of reincarnation, and attain the perfection of life—love of God and a place in His kingdom.

CHAPTER 1

GOD AND THE LAW OF KARMA

Among the vast ancient Sanskrit writings known as the Vedas, the 108 Upaniṣads contain the philosophical essence. And among all the Upaniṣads, the Īśopaniṣad is considered the foremost. In the following essay, based on talks Śrīla Prabhupāda gave on the Īśopaniṣad in 1968, we learn the truth about the Supreme Lord, the laws governing His material and spiritual energies, and how to break free of the bondage of karma.

The *Īśopaniṣad* states that the Supreme Personality of Godhead is "perfect and complete." Part of the Lord's complete arrangement for this material world is his process of creation, maintenance, and destruction. Every living being in this material world has a fixed schedule of six changes: birth, growth, maintenance, the production of by-products, diminution, and destruction. This is the law of material nature. A flower is born as a bud. It grows, remains fresh for two or three days, produces a seed, gradually withers, and then is finished. You cannot stop this by your so-called material science. To try to do so is *avidyā,* ignorance.

Sometimes people foolishly think that by scientific advancement man will become immortal. This is nonsense. You cannot stop the material laws. Therefore in the *Bhagavad-gītā* (7.14) Lord Kṛṣṇa says that the material energy is *duratyayā,* impossible to overcome by material means.

Material nature consists of three modes, *or guṇas: sattva-guṇa, rajo-guṇa,* and *tamo-guṇa,* or the modes of goodness, passion, and ignorance. Another meaning of *guṇa* is "rope." Rope is made by twisting fiber in a threefold process. First the fiber is twisted in three small strands, then three of them are twisted together, then again three of those are twisted together. In this way the rope becomes very strong. Similarly, the three modes of nature—goodness, passion, and ignorance—are mixed, after which they produce some by-product. Then they are mixed again, and then again. Thus they are "twisted together" innumerable times.

In this way the material energy binds you more and more. By your own efforts you cannot get out of this bondage, which is known as *pavarga. Pa-varga* is the fifth set of letters in the Sanskrit Devanāgarī alphabet. It contains the letters *pa, pha, ba, bha,* and *ma. Pa* stands for *pariśrama,* "hard labor." Every living entity in this world is struggling very hard to maintain himself and survive. This is called the hard struggle for existence. *Pha* stands for *phena*, "foam." When a horse works very hard, foam comes out of its mouth. Similarly, when we are tired from working very hard, our tongue may become dry and some foam forms in our mouth. Everyone is working very hard for sense gratification—so much so that foam is coming from their mouth. *Ba* represents *bandha,* "bondage." In spite of all our efforts, we remain bound up by the ropes of the material modes of nature. *Bha* stands for *bhaya*, "fear." In material life, one is always in a blazing fire of fear, since no one knows what will happen next. And ma represents *mṛtyu,* "death." All our hopes and plans for happiness and security in this world are ended by death.

So, Kṛṣṇa consciousness nullifies this *pavarga* process. In other words, by taking to Kṛṣṇa consciousness one attains *apavarga,* where there is no hard struggle for existence and no material bondage, fear, or death. *Pavarga* symptomizes this material world, but when you add the prefix "*a*" to *pavarga,* that means it is nullified. Our Kṛṣṇa consciousness movement is the path of *apavarga.*

Unfortunately, people do not know of these things, and therefore they are wasting their lives. This modern civilization is a soul-killing civilization; people are killing themselves because they do not know what real life is. They are simply living like animals. The animal does not know what life is, so he simply works under the laws of nature, undergoing gradual evolution. But when you get this human form of life, you have a responsibility to live in a different way. Here is a chance for you to become Kṛṣṇa conscious and solve all problems. But if you don't—if you continue to act like animals—you will again have to enter the cycle of birth and death and transmigrate through

8,400,000 species of life. It will take many, many millions of years to come back to the human form of life. For example, the sunshine you are seeing now you will not see again until after twenty-four hours. Everything in nature moves in a cycle. So if you lose this opportunity of elevating yourself, then again you must enter the cycle of transmigration. Nature's law is very strong. Therefore we are opening so many centers so that people may take advantage of this International Society for Krishna Consciousness and elevate themselves.

It is important to take to Kṛṣṇa consciousness immediately, because we do not know how much time is left before death. When your time in this body expires, no one can stop your death. The arrangement of material nature is so strong. You cannot say, "Let me remain." Actually, people sometimes request like that. When I was in Allahabad, an old friend who was very rich was dying. At that time he begged the doctor, "Can't you give me at least four more years to live? I have some plans which I could not finish." You see. This is foolishness. Everyone thinks, "Oh, I have to do this. I have to do that." No. Neither the doctors nor the scientists can check death: "Oh, no, sir. Not four years, not even four minutes. You have to go immediately." This is the law. So before that moment comes, one should be very careful to become realized in Kṛṣṇa consciousness. You should realize Kṛṣṇa consciousness very quickly. Before your next death comes, you must finish your business. That is intelligence. Otherwise you will suffer defeat.

The *Īśopaniṣad* states that whatever emanates from the complete whole—the Supreme Lord—is also complete in itself. Therefore if you want to take advantage of your life and become Kṛṣṇa conscious, there is complete facility. But you have to come to the point of taking up the practice. Kṛṣṇa consciousness is not theoretical; it is practical. All experiments have already been performed. So, as indicated in the *Īśopaniṣad,* there is a complete facility for the small complete units—ourselves—to realize the supreme complete, Kṛṣṇa. We are complete units, but we are small. For example, in a big machine there is a small screw, and the perfection of that small screw is to be fitted in its proper place. Then it has value. But if it becomes unscrewed from the machine and falls down on the floor, it has no value. Similarly, we are perfect as long as we are attached to Kṛṣṇa; otherwise we are useless.

To realize the complete means to realize what our relationship with the complete is. And all forms of incompleteness are experienced only on account of incomplete knowledge of the complete. We are thinking, "I am equal to God. I am God." This is incomplete knowledge. But if you know, "I am part and parcel of God, and therefore I am equal to God in *quality*," that is complete knowledge. The human form of life is a chance to revive the complete manifestation of the consciousness of the living being. You can revive this complete consciousness by the process of Kṛṣṇa consciousness. But if you don't take advantage of this complete facility, you are killing yourself, committing suicide. As it is said in the *Īśopaniṣad,* "The killer of the soul, whoever he may be, must enter into the planets known as the worlds of the faithless, full of darkness and ignorance. " So don't be the killer of your soul. Utilize the complete facility of your human life to become Kṛṣṇa conscious. That is your only business.

Breaking the Bonds of Karma

In conditioned life we are committing sins at every step, even without knowing it. The reason we are sinning unknowingly is that we have been in ignorance from our very birth. This ignorance is prominent despite so many educational institutions. Why? Because despite so many big, big universities, none of them is teaching *ātma-tattva,* the science of the soul. Therefore people remain in ignorance, and they continue to sin and suffer the reactions. That is stated in the *Śrīmad-Bhāgavatam* (5.5.3): *parābhavas tāvad abodha-jāto yāvan na jijñāsata ātma-tattvam.* This foolishness will continue until one comes to the platform of understanding self-realization. Otherwise, all these universities and institutions for imparting knowledge are a continuation of that same ignorance and foolishness. Unless one comes to the point of asking "What am I? What is God? What is this world? What is my relationship with God and this world?" and finds proper answers, one continues to be foolish like an animal and is subjected to transmigration from one body to another in different species of life. This is the result of ignorance.

So, the modern civilization is very risky. One may feel comfortable as a successful businessman or politician, or one may think oneself comfortable because of being born in a rich nation like America, but these statuses of life are temporary. They will have to change, and we do not know what kind of miseries we will have to suffer in our next life because of our sinful activities. So if one does not begin cultivating transcendental knowledge, then one's life is very risky. Suppose a healthy man is living in a contaminated place. Is his life not at risk? He may become infected by disease at any moment. Therefore we should work to dissipate our ignorance through cultivation of transcendental knowledge.

A good example of how we commit sins unknowingly is eating. In the *Bhagavad-gītā* (3.13) Kṛṣṇa says that His devotees are freed from sin because they eat only the remnants of food that has been offered to Him. But, He says, those who cook for themselves eat only sin. The difference between cooking here in this temple and cooking in some ordinary house is that our cooking and eating are relieving us from sin, while the cooking and eating of a nondevotee are simply entangling him more and more in sin. The cooking and eating appear the same, but they are different. Here there is no sin because the food is being cooked and eaten for Kṛṣṇa.

Anything you do outside the field of Kṛṣṇa conscious activities entangles you in the modes of nature. Generally, you are being implicated in sinful activities. Those who are a little more cautious avoid sinful activities and perform pious activities. But one who performs pious activities is also entangled. If a man is pious, he may take birth in a family that is very rich or aristocratic, or he may be very beautiful or get the opportunity to become very learned. These are the results of pious activities. But whether you are pious or impious, you have to enter into the womb of some mother. And that tribulation is very severe. That we have forgotten. Whether you take birth in a very rich and aristocratic family or from an animal womb, the pangs of birth, old age, disease, and death continue.

The Kṛṣṇa consciousness movement is meant to give you an opportunity to solve these four problems—birth, old age, disease, and death. But if you continue to act sinfully and eat sinfully, then these miseries will continue. Otherwise, you can nullify your sinful reactions by surrendering to Kṛṣṇa, as He states in the *Bhagavad-gītā* (18.66): "Just give up all your so-called religious practices and surrender unto Me. I shall protect you from all your sinful reactions." Part of surrendering to Kṛṣṇa is being careful not to eat anything that has not been offered to Him. That should be our determination. Even if we have committed some sin, by eating *prasādam*, food offered to Kṛṣṇa, we will counteract it. If we surrender to Kṛṣṇa in this way, He will protect us from sinful reactions. That is His promise.

And where does a surrendered devotee go at the time of death? Is he finished, as the voidists say? No. Kṛṣṇa says, *mām eti*: "He comes to Me." And what is the benefit of going there? *Mām upetya punar janma duḥkhālayam aśāśvatam nāpnuvanti*: "One who comes back to Me does not have to return to this miserable material world." That is the highest perfection.

The *Īśopaniṣad* states, "The killer of the soul, whoever he may be, must enter into the planets known as the worlds of the faithless, full of darkness and ignorance." Kṛṣṇa is a lion to the demons and a lamb to the devotees. The atheists say, "We have not seen Kṛṣṇa." Yes, you will see Kṛṣṇa—you will see Him as the lion of death when He ultimately comes to capture you: "Ow!" The atheist sees Kṛṣṇa as death. And the theist, or devotee, sees Kṛṣṇa as his lover, as gentle as a lamb.

Actually, everyone is engaged in Kṛṣṇa's service, either out of love or by force. One who is entangled in material life is engaged in Kṛṣṇa's service because he is forced to serve Kṛṣṇa's external, material energy. It is just like what we see with the citizens of the state: whether one is a law-abiding citizen or a criminal, one is subservient to the state. The criminal may say he doesn't care for the state, but then the police will force him to accept the authority of the state by putting him in prison.

Therefore, whether one accepts or rejects Caitanya Mahāprabhu's philosophy that every living entity is eternally the servant of Kṛṣṇa, one remains His servant. The only difference is that the atheist is being forced to accept Kṛṣṇa as his master, and the devotee is voluntarily offering Him service. This Kṛṣṇa consciousness movement is teaching people that they are eternal servants of God and should voluntarily offer Him service: "Don't falsely claim that you are God. Oh, you don't care for God? You have to care." The great demon Hiraṇya-kaśipu also didn't care for God, and so God came and killed him. God is seen by the atheist as death, but by the theist as a lover. That is the difference.

If you are a devotee and understand this philosophy of spiritual life, you can live for a moment or you can live for a hundred years—it doesn't matter. Otherwise, what is the use of living? Some trees live for five hundred or five thousand years, but what is the use of such a life, devoid of higher consciousness?

If you know that you are Kṛṣṇa's servant and that everything belongs to Kṛṣṇa, you can live for hundreds of years doing your duties and there will be no karmic reaction. This is confirmed in the *Bhagavad-gītā* (3.9): *yajñārthāt karmaṇo 'nyatra loko 'yaṁ karma-bandhanaḥ.* "Except work for Kṛṣṇa, any work, whether good or bad, will bind you to this material world." If you do good work, you will have so-called enjoyment in your next life—but you will still remain bound up in the cycle of birth and death. And if you do bad work, then you will have to suffer the sinful reactions and also remain bound up in birth and death. But if you work for Kṛṣṇa, there are no such reactions, good or bad, and at the time of death you will return to Kṛṣṇa. This is the only way to break the bonds of *karma.*

Kṛṣṇa, The Controller and Owner of All

In the *Īśopaniṣad,* the word *īśa* is used to describe the Supreme Personality of Godhead. *Īśa* means "controller." Do you think you are controlled or not? Is there any person anywhere within this universe who is not controlled? Can anyone say, "I am not controlled"? Nobody can say that. So if you are controlled, then why do you declare, "I am not controlled, I am independent, I am God"? Why this nonsense? Māyāvādī impersonalists claim, "I am God, you are God, everyone is God." But if they are controlled, how can they be God? Does this make any sense? God is never controlled; He is the supreme controller. So if somebody is controlled, immediately we should know that he is not God.

Of course, some rascals claim that they are not controlled. I know one such rascal who has a society and is preaching, "I am God." But one day I saw him with a toothache; he was moaning, "Ohhh!" So I asked him, "You claim that you are God, the supreme controller, but now you are under the control of a toothache. What kind of God are you?" So if you see someone who claims that he is God or that everyone is God, you should immediately know such a person is a number-one rascal.

Now, this is not to say that the living entities are not controllers to some extent. In the *Bhagavad-gītā* Lord Kṛṣṇa says that the living entities are His superior energy. Why are the living entities superior energy? Because they are conscious, whereas the material energy is not. Therefore the living entities can control the material energy to some extent. For example, all the paraphernalia in this temple has been made from matter: earth, water, fire, and air. But it was a living entity who molded the material energy into this paraphernalia for the purpose of worshiping Kṛṣṇa. Another example: before people came from Europe, this land of America was mostly vacant. The people who lived here before that did not fully exploit it. But the Europeans came and developed it into a country with great industries and roads.

So the superior energy, the living entities, can have some control over the material energy. That Kṛṣṇa explains in the *Bhagavad-gītā* (7.5): *yayedaṁ dhāryate jagat.* The importance of this material world is due to the living entities. A big city like Los Angeles, New York, or London is valuable as long as the living entities are there. Similarly, the body is valuable as long as the living entity—the soul—is there. Therefore the soul is superior to matter. But that superiority is being misused to exploit matter for sense gratification. That is conditioned life. We have forgotten that, although we are superior to matter, we are still subordinate to God.

The people of the modern civilization do not care for God because they are intoxicated with their superiority over matter. They are simply trying to exploit matter in different ways. But they are forgetting that all people—American, Russian, Chinese, Indian—are subordinate to God. They have forgotten Kṛṣṇa and want to enjoy this material world. That is their disease.

So, the duty of the devotee of the Lord is to invoke the people's Kṛṣṇa consciousness. The devotee explains to them: "You are superior to matter, but you are subordinate to Kṛṣṇa. Therefore you should not try to enjoy matter but rather use it for His enjoyment." For example, we have decorated this temple not for our sense gratification but for Kṛṣṇa's pleasure. What is the difference between us and ordinary people? They are decorating their apartment very nicely, and we are decorating our place very nicely—but the purpose is different. We are doing it for Kṛṣṇa, and they are doing it for themselves. Whether you decorate your personal apartment or Kṛṣṇa's temple, your superiority over matter remains, since you are utilizing matter for your purposes. But when you apply your intelligence toward utilizing matter for Kṛṣṇa's pleasure, your life is successful, whereas when you apply the same intelligence for your sense gratification, you become entangled in material nature and feel anxiety. Then you have to change bodies, one after another.

Kṛṣṇa is the supreme controller of both the inferior energy, matter, and the superior energy, the *jīvātmā*—ourselves. We are Kṛṣṇa's superior energy because we can control the material world, but that control is also conditional. We have only limited control over this material world. But Kṛṣṇa has control over us; therefore, whatever control we have, He has sanctioned. For example, a human being has manufactured this nice microphone using his intelligence. That means he has been able to control matter to a certain degree to fulfill his desires. But where has his intelligence come from? Kṛṣṇa has given man his superior intelligence. In the *Bhagavad-gītā* (15.15) Kṛṣṇa says, *sarvasya cāhaṁ hṛdi sanniviṣṭo mattaḥ smṛtir jñānam apohanaṁ ca:* "I am seated in everyone's heart, and from Me come remembrance, knowledge, and forgetfulness." Therefore the supreme controller is giving intelligence to the superior energy in the human form of body: "Do this. Now do that..." This direction is not whimsical. The person wanted to do something in his past life, but in his present life he forgets, and so Kṛṣṇa reminds him: "You wanted to do this.

Here is an opportunity." So although you have superior intelligence, that is also controlled by Kṛṣṇa. If Kṛṣṇa gives you the intelligence, you can manufacture this nice microphone. Otherwise, you cannot. Therefore in every sphere of life we are controlled by Kṛṣṇa.

We can also see Kṛṣṇa's control on the universal level. For example, there are so many huge planets; this earth planet is only a small one. Still, on this planet there are big oceans like the Atlantic and Pacific, as well as big mountains and skyscraper buildings. Yet despite all this load, the earth is floating in the air just like a swab of cotton. Who is floating it? Can you float even a grain of sand in the air? You may talk about the law of gravity and so many other things, but you cannot control it. Your airplane is flying in the air, but as soon as the petrol is finished, it will immediately fall. So if it takes so many scientists to build an airplane that can float only temporarily in the air, is it possible that this huge earth is floating of its own accord? No. Lord Kṛṣṇa declares in the *Bhagavad-gītā* (15.13), "I enter into the material planets and keep them aloft." Just as to keep an airplane aloft a pilot has to enter it, so to keep this earth aloft Kṛṣṇa has entered it. This is the simple truth.

We have to take knowledge from Kṛṣṇa. We shouldn't accept any process of gaining knowledge except hearing from Kṛṣṇa or His representative. Then we will have first-class knowledge. If you find an authority who is representing Kṛṣṇa and who can speak on the subject matter, and if you accept the knowledge he gives, then your knowledge is perfect. Of all the processes for receiving knowledge, the least reliable is direct sense perception. Suppose someone asks, "Can you show me God?" That means he wants to experience everything directly. But this is a second-class process for gaining knowledge, because our senses are imperfect and we are prone to make mistakes. Suppose you need some gold but you don't know where to purchase it. So you go to a proprietor of a hardware store and ask, "Do you have any gold in stock?" He will immediately understand that you are a first-class fool because you have come to purchase gold in a hardware store. Therefore he will try to cheat you. He will give you a piece of iron and say, "Here is gold." Then what will you say? Will you accept that iron as gold? Because you do not know what gold is and have gone to a hardware store to purchase it, you will get a piece of iron and be cheated. Similarly, rascals who demand that they be shown God do not know what God is, and therefore they are being cheated by so many bogus spiritual leaders who claim that they are God. That is happening.

If you want to purchase gold, you must have at least some preliminary knowledge of what gold is. Similarly, if you want to see God, the first requirement is that you must know some of the basic characteristics of God. Otherwise, if you go to some rascal and he claims to be God and you accept him as God, you will be cheated.

Another question we should ask when someone says "I want to see God" is, "What qualification do you have to see God?" God is not so cheap that He can be seen by anybody and everybody. No, the Kṛṣṇa consciousness movement does not present any nonsense or cheap thing. If you want to see God face to face, then you must follow the rules and regulations. You must chant Hare Kṛṣṇa and purify yourself. Then gradually the time will come when you are purified and you will see God.

Still, even though in your present contaminated condition you are not qualified to see God, He is so kind that He allows you to see Him in His Deity form in the temple. In that form He agrees to be seen by everyone, whether or not one knows He is God. The Deity is not an idol; it is not imagination. The knowledge of how to construct the Deity and install Him on the altar is received from the scripture and the superior *ācāryas,* or spiritual masters. Therefore the authorized Deity in the temple is Kṛṣṇa Himself and can fully reciprocate your love and service.

With your present blunt material senses, however, you cannot immediately perceive God's spiritual form, name, qualities, pastimes, and paraphernalia. And because people in the present civilization have no power to understand God and are not guided by some person who can help them understand God, they have become godless. But if you read Vedic scriptures like the *Īśopaniṣad* and *Bhagavad-gītā* under superior guidance and follow the rules and regulations, eventually God will be revealed to you. You cannot see God or understand God by your own endeavor. You have to surrender to the process by which God can be known. Then He will reveal Himself. He is the supreme controller; you are being controlled. So how can you control God? "O God, come here. I want to see You." God is not so cheap that by your order He will come and be seen by you. No, that is not possible. You must always remember, "God is the supreme controller and I am controlled. So if I can please God by my service, then He will reveal Himself to me." That is the process of knowing God.

Ultimately, this process leads to love of God. That is real religion. It doesn't matter whether you follow the Hindu, Muslim, or Christian religion: if you are developing love of God, then you are perfect in your religion. And what kind of love should we develop for God? It must be without any selfish motivation—"O Lord, I love you because You supply me so many nice things. You are my order supplier." No, we should not have this sort of love for God. It should not depend on any exchange.

Lord Caitanya Mahāprabhu taught, "O Lord! Whether You trample me under Your feet or embrace me or leave me brokenhearted by not being present before me, that does not matter. You are completely free to do anything, for You are my worshipable Lord unconditionally." That is love. We should think, "God may do whatever He likes, yet I will still love Him. I don't want anything in exchange." That is the sort of love Kṛṣṇa wants. That is why He is so fond of the *gopīs.* In the *gopīs'* love there is no question of business ex-changes—"Give me this, then I will love You." Their love was pure, unalloyed, without any impediment. If you try to love God in this way, nothing in the whole world can check you. You only have to develop your eagerness—"Kṛṣṇa! I want You." That's all. Then there is no question of being stopped. In any condition your love will increase. If you attain that state, you will feel fully satisfied. It is not that God wants you to love Him for His benefit. It is for your benefit. If you do otherwise, you will never be happy.

God and His Energies

The *Īśopaniṣad* explains that whatever we see, whether animate or inanimate, is controlled by the Supreme Lord. Lord Kṛṣṇa says the same thing in the *Bhagavad-gītā* (9.10)—that His energies are managing everything. And the *Viṣṇu Purāṇa confirms, eka-deśa-sthitasyāgner jyotsnā vistārinī yathā:* "As heat and light are distributed all around by a fire situated in one place, so the whole creation is a manifestation of energies expanded from the Supreme Lord." For example, the sun is in one place, but it is distributing its heat and light all over the universe. Similarly, the Supreme Lord is distributing His material and spiritual energies all over the creation.

The spiritual energy is present in this temporary material world, but it is covered by the material energy. For example, the sun is always shining in the sky—no one can stop the sun from shining—but it is sometimes covered by a cloud. When this happens, the sunshine on the ground is dim. The more the sun is covered, the dimmer the sunlight. But this covering of the sun is partial. All the sunshine cannot be covered; that is not possible. An insignificant portion of the sunshine may be covered by a cloud. Similarly, this material world is an insignificant portion of the spiritual world that is covered by the material energy.

And what is the material energy? The material energy is just another form of the spiritual energy. It manifests when there is an absence of spiritual activity. Again the analogy of the sun and the cloud: What is a cloud? It is an effect of the sunshine. The sunshine evaporates water from the sea, and a cloud is formed. So the sun is the cause of the cloud. Similarly, the Supreme Lord is the cause of this material energy, which covers our vision of Him.

In this way, two energies are working in this material world: the spiritual energy and the material energy. The material energy consists of eight material elements: earth, water, fire, air, ether, mind, intelligence, and false ego. These are arranged from the grosser to the finer. Water is finer than earth, fire is finer than water, etc.

So, the finer the element, the more powerful it is. For example, at the speed of the mind you can go many thousands of miles within a second. But even more powerful than the mind is the intelligence, and even more powerful than the intelligence is spiritual energy. What is spiritual energy? That is stated by Kṛṣṇa in the *Bhagavad-gītā* (7.5): *apareyam itas tv anyāṁ prakṛtiṁ viddhi me parām jīva-bhūtām.*

"Beyond My inferior, material energy is another energy, which is spiritual. It comprises the living entities."

We living entities are also energy, but superior energy. How are we superior? Because we can control the inferior energy, matter. Matter has no power to act on its own. The big airplane can fly so nicely in the sky, but unless the spiritual energy—the pilot—is there, it is useless. The jet plane will sit in the airport for thousands of years; it will not fly unless the small particle of spiritual energy, the pilot, comes and touches it. So what is the difficulty in understanding God? If there are so many huge machines that cannot move without the touch of the spiritual energy, a living being, then how can you argue that this whole material energy works automatically, without any control? Who would put forward such a foolish argument? Therefore, those who cannot understand how this material energy is being controlled by the Supreme Lord are less intelligent. The godless men who believe that this material energy is working automatically are fools.

The statement of the *Īśopaniṣad* is that "Everything animate or inanimate is controlled and owned by the Supreme Personality of Godhead." Because He is the supreme controller, He is also the supreme proprietor. In our practical experience we see that the man who controls a business establishment is the proprietor. Similarly, since God is the controller of this material world, He is also its proprietor. This means that as far as possible we should engage everything in the Lord's service.

Then what about our own needs? That is explained in the Īśopaniṣad: "One should accept only those things necessary for himself, which are set aside as his quota, and one should not accept other things, knowing well to whom they belong." Kṛṣṇa consciousness means to understand things as they are. So if we simply understand these principles, we will be well situated in Kṛṣṇa consciousness.

The Position of Kṛṣṇa

The *Īśopaniṣad* states, "Although fixed in His abode, the Personality of Godhead is swifter than the mind and can overcome all others running. The powerful demigods cannot approach Him. Although in one place, He controls those who supply the air and rain. He surpasses all in excellence." The *Brahma-saṁhitā* says something similar: *goloka eva nivasaty akhilātma-bhūtaḥ.* Although Kṛṣṇa is always in Goloka Vṛndāvana, He is simultaneously in the hearts of all living beings.

Kṛṣṇa has no duties to perform in Goloka. He is simply enjoying in the company of His associates—the *gopīs,* the cowherd boys, His mother and father, His cows and calves, etc. He is completely free. And His associates are even freer than He is, because when they seem to be in danger, Kṛṣṇa feels some anxiety about how to save them. But His associates feel no anxiety. They simply think, "Oh, Kṛṣṇa is here. He will protect us." When Kṛṣṇa enacted His pastimes five thousand years ago in Vṛndāvana, India, He would go every day with His cowherd boyfriends and their calves and cows to play in the forest on the bank of the Yamunā River. And often Kaṁsa would send some demon to try to kill Kṛṣṇa and His friends. Yet the cowherd boys would continue enjoying their pastimes without anxiety because they were so confident of Kṛṣṇa's protection. That is spiritual life, which begins with surrendering to Kṛṣṇa.

Surrendering to Kṛṣṇa means having the strong faith that Kṛṣṇa will save us in any dangerous condition. The first step in surrendering is that we should accept whatever is favorable for devotional service. Then we should reject anything that is unfavorable for devotional service. The next stage is the confidence that in any situation Kṛṣṇa will protect us and maintain us. Actually, He is already giving protection and maintenance to everyone. That is a fact. But in *māyā* (illusion) we think that we are protecting ourselves, or that we are feeding ourselves.

For the devotees, Kṛṣṇa personally takes charge of their protection and maintenance. And for the ordinary living entities, Māyā-devī-Kṛṣṇa's external energy-takes charge. Māyā-devī is Kṛṣṇa's agent for punishing the conditioned souls. The situation is like what we see in the state: good citizens are taken care of by the government directly, while criminals are taken care of by the government through the prison department. In the prison house the government takes care that the prisoners get sufficient food, and that they get hospital treatment if they become diseased. The government cares for them—but under punishment.

Similarly, in this material world Kṛṣṇa has certainly arranged for our care, but also for our punishment. If you commit this sin, then slap. If you commit that sin, then kick. This is going on under the heading of the threefold miseries—those caused by our own body and mind, those caused by other living entities, and those caused by natural calamities under the supervision of the demigods. Unfortunately, instead of understanding that we are being punished for sinful activities, under the spell of māyā we are thinking that this kicking, slapping, and thrashing are accidental. This is illusion.

As soon as you take up Kṛṣṇa consciousness, Kṛṣṇa begins personally taking care of you. As He promises in the *Bhagavad-gītā* (18.66), "I will take care of you. I will save you from all sinful reactions. Do not worry." Because we have had so many lives in this material world, we are suffering under heaps of sinful reactions. But as soon as you surrender to Kṛṣṇa, He immediately takes care of you and nullifies all your sinful reactions. Kṛṣṇa says, "Don't hesitate." Don't think, "Oh, I have committed so many sins. How can Kṛṣṇa save me?" No. Kṛṣṇa is all-powerful. He can save you. Your duty is to surrender to Him and without any reservation dedicate your life to His service. Then Kṛṣṇa will save you without a doubt.

Kṛṣṇa: A Seeming Paradox

The *Īśopaniṣad* states, "The Supreme Lord walks and does not walk. He is far away, but He is very near as well. He is within everything, and yet He is outside of everything." How can Kṛṣṇa walk and also not walk? As a crude example, consider how the sun at noontime shines on your head. Now, if you begin walking, you will see that the sun is accompanying you. About forty years ago, when I was a householder, I was once walking with my second son in the evening. He was four years old. All of a sudden he said, "O father, why is the moon following us?" You see? The moon and the sun are fixed in the sky, yet they seem to be moving with us. Similarly, if you are going on an airplane or a train, you will see that the moon or the sun is going with you. So if this is possible for the sun and the moon, why can't Kṛṣṇa also walk with you? "Although He is situated far away, He is very near as well." In other words, although Kṛṣṇa is in Goloka Vṛndāvana enjoying pastimes with His associates, He is simultaneously everywhere in this material world. In this way the Supreme Lord "walks and does not walk."

If Kṛṣṇa were not present here as well as in Goloka, how could He accept the food the devotees offer Him? Don't think that Kṛṣṇa does not accept the devotees' offerings. He can stretch His hand immediately if one offers Him something with devotion. In the *Bhagavad-gītā* (9.26) Kṛṣṇa says, *tad ahaṁ bhakty-upahṛtam aśnāmi:* "Whenever someone offers Me something with faith and love, I accept it." People may ask, "Oh, Kṛṣṇa is far away in Goloka Vṛndāvana. How can He eat your offering?" Yes, He accepts it. Yes, He eats it—provided it is offered with love.

So, Kṛṣṇa is present everywhere, and He can manifest Himself anywhere immediately, but you must have the qualification to call Him. If you are actually a devotee, Kṛṣṇa will immediately come to protect you. The demon Hiraṇyakaśipu challenged his son, the devotee Prahlāda: "Where is your God? You say He is everywhere. Then is He in this column of my palace? You think your God is there? All right. Then I will kill Him." Hiraṇyakaśipu immediately broke the column. Then Kṛṣṇa came out of the column in His form as Nṛsiṁhadeva—half man and half lion—and killed the demon. That is Kṛṣṇa.

So Kṛṣṇa can manifest Himself anywhere because He is present everywhere. That is explained in the *Īśopaniṣad*: *tad antarasya sarvasya tad u sarvasyāsya bāhyataḥ*. "The Supreme Lord is within everything, and yet He is outside of everything as well." This Vedic mantra is proof that the Lord is everywhere. Whatever is said in the *Vedas* is a fact. Unless you accept the *Vedas* as axiomatic truth, you cannot make progress in Kṛṣṇa consciousness. In mathematics there are also many axiomatic truths—a point has no length or breadth, things equal to the same thing are equal to one another, etc. These are axiomatic truths, and we have to accept them if we want to learn mathematics. Similarly, the Vedas contain axiomatic truths, and we have to accept the Vedas as axiomatic if we want to make spiritual progress.

Sometimes the *Vedas* seem to contradict themselves, but still we have to accept all the Vedic injunctions. For example, according to Vedic injunction, if you touch the bone of an animal you immediately become impure and must take a bath. Now, a conchshell is the bone of an animal, but the conchshell is used in the Deity room, where everything must be spotlessly pure. You cannot argue, "Oh, you said that a bone is impure, and that as soon as you touch it you become impure. Still you are putting a conchshell in the Deity room?" No. There is no room for such an argument. You have to accept that while bones are impure, the conchshell is so pure that it can be used in the Deity room.

Similarly, you have to accept the spiritual master's order as axiomatic. There can be no argument. In this way you can make progress. You cannot argue about things that are inconceivable to you. You will only fail. You have to accept the Vedic injunctions and the orders of the spiritual master as axiomatic truth. This is not dogmatic, because our predecessor spiritual masters accepted this principle. If you argue with your spiritual master, you will never reach a conclusion. The argument will go on perpetually: you put some argument, I put some argument... That is not the process.

As the Mahābhārata says, *tarko 'pratiṣṭhaḥ śrutayo vibhinnā:* Mere logic and argument can never come to a firm conclusion, and due to different countries and different circumstances, one scripture is different from another. Then *nāsāv ṛṣir yasya mataṁ na bhinnam*: As far as philosophical speculation is concerned, one philosopher puts forward some theory, then another philosopher puts forward another theory, and the theories always contradict each other. Unless you defeat another philosopher, you cannot be a famous philosopher. That is the way of philosophy. Then how can one learn the conclusive philosophical truth? That is stated: *dharmasya tattvaṁ nihitaṁ guhāyām*. The secret of the religious process is lying within the hearts of the self-realized souls. Then how do you realize it?

Mahājano yena gataḥ sa panthāḥ: You have to follow in the footsteps of great spiritual personalities. Therefore we are trying to follow Lord Kṛṣṇa and Lord Caitanya. That is perfection. You have to accept the injunctions of the Vedas, and you have to follow the instructions of the bona fide spiritual master. Then success is sure.

The Lord and His Energy—One and Different

The *Īśopaniṣad* states, "One who always sees all living entities as spiritual sparks, in quality one with the Lord, becomes a true knower of things. What, then, can cause him illusion or anxiety?" This realization is Kṛṣṇa consciousness. There are different kinds of realization, but the devotee of Kṛṣṇa realizes the truth-that we are qualitatively one with the Lord but quantitatively different from Him. The impersonalists think that we are a hundred percent one with the Lord, or the Supreme Absolute Truth. But that is not a fact. If we were a hundred percent one with the Supreme Lord, then how have we come under the control of *māyā* (illusion)? The impersonalists cannot answer this question.

The real nature of our identity with the Supreme is described in the Vedic literature with the analogy of the sparks and the fire. The sparks of a fire have the same quality as the fire, yet they are different in quantity. But when the small spark leaves the fire and falls down in water, its fiery quality is lost. Similarly, when the infinitesimal soul leaves the association of the Lord and contacts the mode of ignorance, his spiritual quality becomes almost extinct. When a spark falls on the land instead of in the water, then the spark retains some heat. Similarly, when the living entity is in the quality of passion, there is some hope that he can revive his Kṛṣṇa consciousness. And if the spark drops onto dry grass, it can ignite another fire and regain all its fiery qualities. Similarly, a person who is in the mode of goodness can take full advantage of spiritual association and easily revive his Kṛṣṇa consciousness. Therefore one has to come to the platform of goodness in this material world.

Again, the analogy of the fire can help us understand the simultaneous oneness and difference of the Lord and His diverse energies. Fire has two main energies, heat and light. Wherever there is fire, there is heat and light. Now, the heat is not different from the fire, nor is the light—but still, heat and light are not fire. Similarly, the whole universe can be understood in this way. The universe is simply made up of Kṛṣṇa's energies, and therefore nothing is different from Kṛṣṇa. But still, Kṛṣṇa is separate from everything in the material universe.

So, whatever we see within the material or spiritual worlds is but an expansion of Kṛṣṇa's multifarious energies. This material world is an expansion of Kṛṣṇa's external energy (*bahiraṅgā śakti*), the spiritual world is an expansion of His internal energy (*antaraṅgā śakti*), and we living entities are an expansion of His marginal energy (*taṭasthā śakti*). We are śakti, energy. We are not the energetic.

The Māyāvādī philosophers say that because the energies are not outside of Brahman, the energetic, they are all identical with Brahman. This is monism. Our Vaiṣṇava philosophy is that the energy is simultaneously one with and different from the energetic. Again the analogy of the heat and fire: When you perceive heat, you understand that there is fire nearby. But this does not mean that because you feel some heat, you are in the fire. So the heat and the fire, the energy and the energetic, are one yet different.

So the Māyāvāda philosophy of oneness and our Vaiṣṇava philosophy of oneness are different. The Māyā-vādīs say Brahman is real but that the energy emanating from Brahman is false. We say that because Brahman is real, His energy must also be real. That is the difference between Māyāvāda philosophy and Vaiṣṇava philosophy. One cannot claim that this material energy is false, although it is certainly temporary. Suppose we have some trouble. There are so many kinds of trouble pertaining to the body and mind and external affairs. That trouble comes and goes, but when we are undergoing it, it is certainly real. We feel the consequence. We cannot say it is false. The Māyāvādī philosophers say that it is false. But then why do they become so disturbed when they have some trouble? No, none of Kṛṣṇa's energies is false.

The *Īśopaniṣad* uses the word *vijānataḥ*—"one who knows"—to describe a person who understands the oneness and difference of the Lord and His energies. If one is not *vijānataḥ,* one will remain in illusion and suffer. But for one who knows, there is no illusion, no lamentation. When you are perfectly convinced that there is nothing except Kṛṣṇa and Kṛṣṇa's energies, then there is no illusion or lamentation for you. This is known as the brahma-bhūta stage, as explained in the *Bhagavad-gītā* (18.54): *brahma-bhūtaḥ prasannātmā na śocati na kāṅkṣati.* "One who is transcendentally situated in Brahman realization becomes fully joyful, and he never laments or desires to have anything."

For our sense gratification we are very eager to get things we do not have. That is hankering. And when we lose something, we lament. But if we know that Kṛṣṇa is the source and proprietor of the entire material energy, we understand that everything belongs to Him and that anything gained is given by Him for His service. Thus we do not hanker for the things of this world. Furthermore, if something is taken away by Kṛṣṇa, then what is the need for lamentation? We should think, "Kṛṣṇa wanted to take it away from me. Therefore, why should I lament? The Supreme Lord is the cause of all causes. He takes away, He also gives." When one is thus in full knowledge, there is no more lamentation and no more hankering. That is the spiritual platform. Then you can see everyone as a spiritual spark, as part and parcel of Kṛṣṇa, and as His eternal servant.

Kṛṣṇa, The Supreme Pure

The *Īśopaniṣad* states that the Lord is "the greatest of all, unembodied, omniscient, beyond reproach, without veins, pure and uncontaminated." No sin can pollute Kṛṣṇa. Sometimes less intelligent persons criticize Kṛṣṇa: "Why did Kṛṣṇa engage in the *rāsa* dance, enjoying with other men's wives in the middle of the night?" Kṛṣṇa is God. He can do whatever He likes. Your laws cannot restrict Kṛṣṇa. For you there are so many restrictive laws, but for Kṛṣṇa there is no restrictive law. He can surpass all regulations.

Parīkṣit Mahārāja asked this same question of Śukadeva Gosvāmī: "Kṛṣṇa came to establish the principles of morality and religion. Then why did He enjoy the company of so many young girls who were the wives of others? This seems to be very sinful." Śukadeva

Gosvāmī answered that Kṛṣṇa cannot be contaminated by sin; rather, whoever comes in contact with Kṛṣṇa, even with a contaminated mind, becomes purified. The sun is a good analogy: the sun cannot be contaminated; rather, if something contaminated is placed in the sunshine, it becomes purified. Similarly, you may approach Kṛṣṇa with any material desire and you will become purified. Of course, the gopīs' feelings toward Kṛṣṇa are not at all material. Still, as young girls they were captivated by His beauty. They approached Kṛṣṇa with the desire to have Him as their paramour. But actually, they became purified. Even demons can become purified by coming in contact with Kṛṣṇa. The demon Kaṁsa, for example, thought of Kṛṣṇa as his enemy. But he was also Kṛṣṇa conscious, always thinking, "Oh, how will I find Kṛṣṇa? I will kill Him." That was his demoniac mentality. But he also became purified. He got salvation.

The conclusion is that if we can somehow or other develop our Kṛṣṇa consciousness, we will immediately become purified of all sinful desires. Kṛṣṇa gives this chance to everyone.

Beyond the Limits of the Body

When the *Īśopaniṣad* describes the Supreme Lord as "He who is the greatest of all, who is unembodied and omniscient," this shows the distinction between God and ourselves. We are embodied. Therefore my body is different from me. When I leave this body, it becomes dust. As the Bible says, "Dust thou art, and unto dust shalt thou return." But I am not dust; I am a spirit soul. Therefore *thou* means "the body."

Kṛṣṇa, however, is not embodied. This means there is no difference between His body and His soul. In other words, His body is pure spirit. Therefore He does not change His body. And because He does not change His body, He is omniscient—He remembers everything. Because we do change our material bodies, however, we forget what happened in our last birth. We have forgotten who we were, just as when we sleep we forget our body and our surroundings. The body becomes tired and rests; it becomes inactive. In contrast, in a dreamland I work, I go somewhere, I fly, I create another body, another environment. This we experience every night. It is not difficult to understand.

Similarly, in every life we create a different environment. In this life I may think I am an Indian. In my next life, however, I may not be an Indian—I may be an American. But even if I become an American, I may not be a man. I may be a cow or a bull. Then I would be sent to the slaughterhouse. Do you see the difficulty?

The problem is that we are always changing bodies, life after life. It is a serious problem. We have no fixed position; we do not know where we will be placed within the 8,400,000 species of life. But there is a solution: If somehow or other a person develops pure Kṛṣṇa consciousness, he will go to Kṛṣṇa at the time of death, and then he does not have to accept a material body again. He gets a spiritual body similar to Kṛṣṇa's, full of eternity, knowledge, and bliss.

Therefore we should take up the practice of Kṛṣṇa consciousness and execute it very seriously, without any deviation. We should not think that Kṛṣṇa consciousness is some kind of fashion. No, it is the most important function of every human being. Human life is simply meant for developing Kṛṣṇa consciousness. One has no other business.

Unfortunately, the people of the modern civilization have created so many other engagements that they are forgetting Kṛṣṇa consciousness. This is called māyā, or illusion. They are forgetting their real business. And the rascal, blind leaders are leading everyone to hell. They are simply *mis*leaders. People do not like to accept any authority. Still, they have accepted these rascals as leaders and are being misled. In this way both the rascal leaders and their unfortunate followers remain bound up by the stringent laws of material nature.

So, if somehow or other one comes in contact with Kṛṣṇa, one should seriously take up the process of Kṛṣṇa consciousness and catch hold of His lotus feet very tightly. If you hold on to Kṛṣṇa's lotus feet very tightly, *māyā* will not be able to harm you.

Spiritual and Material Education

The *Īśopaniṣad* states, "Those who are engaged in the culture of nescience shall enter into the darkest region of ignorance. " There are two kinds of education, material and spiritual. Material education is called *jaḍa-vidyā. Jaḍa* means "that which cannot move," or matter. Spirit can move. Our body is a combination of spirit and matter. As long as the spirit is there, the body is moving. For example, a man's coat and pants move as long as the man wears them. It appears that the coat and pants are moving on their own, but actually it is the body that is moving them. Similarly, this body is moving because the spirit soul is moving it. Another example is the motorcar. The motorcar is moving because the driver is moving it. Only a fool thinks the motorcar is moving on its own. In spite of a wonderful mechanical arrangement, the motorcar cannot move on its own.

Since they are given only *jaḍa-vidyā,* a materialistic education, people think that this material nature is working, moving, and manifesting so many wonderful things automatically. When we are at the seaside, we see the waves moving. But the waves are not moving automatically. The air is moving them. And something else is moving the air. In this way, if you go all the way back to the ultimate cause, you will find Kṛṣṇa, the cause of all causes. That is real education, to search out the ultimate cause.

So the *Īśopaniṣad* says that those who are captivated by the external movements of the material energy are worshiping nescience. In the modern civilization there are big, big institutions for understanding technology, how a motorcar or an airplane moves. They are studying how to manufacture so much machinery. But there is no educational institution for investigating how the spirit soul is moving. The actual mover is not being studied. Instead they are studying the external movements of matter.

When I lectured at the Massachusetts Institute of Technology, I asked the students, "Where is the technology to study the soul, the mover of the body?" They had no such technology. They could not answer satisfactorily because their education was simply *jaḍa-vidyā*. The *Īśopaniṣad* says that those who engage in the advancement of such materialistic education will go to the darkest region of existence. Therefore the present civilization is in a very dangerous position because there is no arrangement anywhere in the world for genuine spiritual education. In this way human society is being pushed to the darkest region of existence.

In a song, Śrīla Bhaktivinoda Ṭhākura has declared that materialistic education is simply an expansion of *māyā*. The more we advance in this materialistic education, the more our ability to understand God will be hampered. And at last we will declare, "God is dead." This is all ignorance and darkness.

So, the materialists are certainly being pushed into darkness. But there is another class—the so-called philosophers, mental speculators, religionists, and *yogīs*—who are going into still greater darkness because they are defying Kṛṣṇa. They are pretending to cultivate spiritual knowledge, but because they have no information of Kṛṣṇa, or God, their teachings are even more dangerous than those of the outright materialists. Why? Because they are misleading people into thinking they are giving real spiritual knowledge. The so-called *yoga* system they are teaching is misleading people: "Simply meditate, and you will understand that you are God." Kṛṣṇa never meditated to become God. He was God from His very birth. When He was a three-month-old baby, the Pūtanā demon attacked Him—and Kṛṣṇa sucked out her life air along with her breast milk. So Kṛṣṇa was God from the very beginning. That is God.

The nonsense so-called *yogīs* teach, "You become still and silent, and you will become God." How can I become silent? Is there any possibility of becoming silent? No, there is no such possibility. "Become desireless and you will become God." How can I become desireless? These are all bluffs. We cannot be desireless. We cannot be silent. But our desires and our activities can be purified. That is real knowledge. We should desire only to serve Kṛṣṇa. That is purification of desire. Instead of trying to be still and silent, we should dovetail our activities in Kṛṣṇa's service. As living entities, we have activities, desires, and a loving propensity, but they are being misdirected. If we direct them into Kṛṣṇa's service, that is the perfection of education.

We don't say that you should not become advanced in material education. You may, but at the same time you should become Kṛṣṇa conscious. That is our message. We don't say that you shouldn't manufacture motorcars. No. We say, "All right, you have manufactured these motorcars. Now employ them in Kṛṣṇa's service." That is our proposal.

So education is required, but if it is simply materialistic—if it is devoid of Kṛṣṇa consciousness—it is very, very dangerous. That is the teaching of the *Īśopaniṣad.*

Knowledge Vs. Nescience

The *Īśopaniṣad* says, "The wise have explained that one result is derived from the culture of knowledge and that a different result is obtained from the culture of nescience." As explained above, the real culture of knowledge is the advancement of spiritual knowledge. And advancement of knowledge in the matter of bodily comforts or to protect the body is the culture of nescience, because however you may try to protect this body, it will follow its natural course. What is that? Repeated birth and death, and while the body is manifested, disease and old age. People are very busy cultivating knowledge of this body, although they see that at every moment the body is decaying. The death of the body was fixed when it was born. That is a fact. So you cannot stop the natural course of this body—namely birth, old age, disease, and death.

The *Śrīmad-Bhāgavatam* (10.84.13) says that this body is nothing but a bag containing three primary elements—mucus, bile, and air—and that one who accepts this combination of mucus, bile, and air as himself is an ass. Even great philosophers and scientists take themselves to be this combination of mucus, bile, and air. This is their mistake. Actually, the philosophers and scientists are spirit souls, and according to their *karma* they are exhibiting their talent. They do not understand the law of *karma.*

Why do we find so many different personalities? If human beings are nothing but combinations of mucus, bile, and air, why are they not identical? One man is born a millionaire; another is unable to have two full meals a day, despite struggling very hard. Why this difference? Because of the law of *karma,* action and reaction. One who understands this mystery is in knowledge.

Human life is meant for understanding the mystery of life. And one who fails to utilize this human form for this purpose is a *kṛpaṇa,* a miser. This is stated in the *Garga Upaniṣad.* If you get one million dollars and do not use it, thinking, "Oh, I will simply keep this bank balance of one million dollars," you are a *kṛpaṇa.* You do not know how to use your money. On the other hand, one who uses his million dollars to make another million dollars is intelligent. Similarly, this human body is invaluable. One who uses it for cultivating spiritual knowledge is a *brāhmaṇa,* a wise man, and one who cultivates materialistic knowledge is a kṛpaṇa, a miser. That is the difference between *brāhmaṇa* and *kṛpaṇa.*

One who uses this body the way cats and dogs do—for sense gratification—is a miser. He does not know how to use his "million dollars." Therefore it is the duty of the father, the mother, the state, and the teachers to provide spiritual education for their dependents from the very beginning of their lives. Indeed, the *Śrīmad-Bhāgavatam* says that one should not become a father, a mother, a teacher, or a governmental head unless one is able to elevate one's dependents to the platform of spiritual knowledge, which can save them from repeated birth and death.

THE WAY OF KNOWING GOD

In the Vedic disciplic succession, the spiritual masters always base their statements on what they have heard from authoritative sources, never on personal experience. Trying to understand things by one's own direct experience is the material process of gaining knowledge, technically called *pratyakṣa.* The Vedic method is different. It is called *śruti*, which means "to hear from authoritative sources." That is the secret of Vedic understanding.

With your imperfect senses you should not try to understand things that are beyond your experimental powers. That is not possible. Suppose you want to know who your father is. Can you find out by experimenting? Is it possible? No. Then how can you know who your father is? By hearing from the proper authority, your mother. This is common sense. And if you cannot know your material father by the experimental process, how can you know the Supreme Father by the experimental process? Kṛṣṇa is the original father. He is the father of the father of the father, all the way down to you. So if you cannot understand your immediate father, the previous generation, by the experimental process, how can you know God, or Kṛṣṇa, in this way?

People search for God by the experimental process, but after much searching they fail. Then they say, "Oh, there is no God. I am God." But the *Īśopaniṣad* says that one should try to learn about God not by the experimental process but by hearing. From whom should one hear? From a shopkeeper? From fanatics? No. One should hear from those who are *dhīra*. *Dhīra* means "one whose senses are not agitated by material influence."

There are different kinds of agitation—agitations of the mind, the power of speech, and anger, and agitations of the tongue, belly, and genitals. When we become angry, we forget everything and can do any nonsense and speak so much nonsense. For the agitation of the tongue there are so many advertisements: "Here is liquor, here is chicken, here is beef." Will we die without liquor, chicken, or beef? No. For the human beings Kṛṣṇa has given so many nice things to eat—grains, fruits, milk, and so on.

The cow produces milk abundantly, not for herself but for human beings. That is proper human food. God says, "Mrs. Cow, although you are producing milk, you cannot drink it. It is for the human beings, who are more advanced than animals." Of course, in the infant stage animals live off their mother's milk, so the calves drink some of the cow's milk. But the cow gives excess milk, and that excess is specifically meant for us.

We should accept whatever God has ordained as our proper food. But no, because of the agitation of the tongue, we think, "Why should I be satisfied eating grains, milk products, vegetables, and fruits? Let me maintain a slaughterhouse and kill these cows. After drinking their milk, just as I drank my mother's milk, let me kill them to satisfy my tongue." You shouldn't think such nonsense but should hear from the *dhīras,* or *svāmīs,* who have controlled their senses. A *svāmī,* or *gosvāmī,* is one who has control over the six agitations: the speech, the mind, anger, the tongue, the belly, and the genitals.

There is a nice poem by Kālidāsa called *Kumāra-sambhava* describing how Lord Śiva is *dhīra*. When Lord Śiva's wife, Satī, heard Śiva being blasphemed at a sacrifice performed by her father, she committed suicide. Upon hearing about his wife's suicide, Lord Śiva became very angry and left this planet to meditate elsewhere. During that time there was a war between the demons and the demigods. The demigods needed a good general. They concluded that if Lord Śiva were to beget a son, the son would be able to lead them in the fight against the demons. Lord Śiva was completely naked while meditating. So Pārvatī, the reincarnation of Satī, was sent to agitate his genitals for sex. But he was not agitated. He remained silent. At this point Kālidāsa remarks, "Here is a *dhīra.* He is naked, and a young girl is touching his genitals, but still he is not agitated."

Dhīra means that even if there is some cause for agitation, one will not be agitated. If there is some very nice food, my tongue should not be agitated to taste it. If there is a very nice girl or boy, still I should not be agitated sexually. In this way one who is *dhīra* is able to control the six agitating forces mentioned above. It is not that Lord Śiva was impotent: he was *dhīra.* Similarly, Kṛṣṇa danced with so many girls, but there was no sex appetite.

So, you have to hear from a person who is *dhīra.* If you hear from the *adhīra,* from those who are not self-controlled, then whatever knowledge you learn will be useless. In the *Īśopaniṣad,* a student has approached his spiritual master to inquire from him, and the spiritual master is saying, "This is what I have heard from authoritative sources." The spiritual master is not inventing something from his own experience. He is presenting exactly what he has heard.

So we have nothing to research. Everything is there. We simply have to hear from a person who is *dhīra,* who is not agitated by the six urges. That is the Vedic process of gaining knowledge. And if we try to use some other process, we will remain covered by nescience.

The *Īśopaniṣad* states, "Only one who can learn the process of nescience and that of transcendental knowledge side by side can transcend the influence of repeated birth and death and enjoy the full blessings of immortality." People do not understand what immortality is. They think it is a mythological idea. They are proud of their advancement of knowledge, but there are many things they do not know, nor can they ever know them by their modern system of experimentation.

So if you want real knowledge, you should take knowledge from the literature known as the *Vedas.* (The word *veda* means "knowledge.") Part of the *Vedas* are the 108 *Upaniṣads,* out of which eleven are very important. Of those eleven, the *Īśopaniṣad* stands first. In the word *upaniṣad*, upa means "near." So the knowledge in the *Īśopaniṣad* will take you nearer to Kṛṣṇa.

In learned society the *Vedas* are accepted as śruti, or primary evidence. The *Vedas* are not knowledge established by the research work of contaminated, conditioned souls. Such people have imperfect senses, and so they cannot see things as they are. They simply theorize, "It may be like this. It may be like that." That is not knowledge. Knowledge is definite, without any doubt or mistake. Conditioned souls commit mistakes, become illusioned, and cheat. How do they cheat? When one who does not understand the *Bhagavad-gītā* writes a commentary on it, he is cheating the innocent public. Someone has a title as a scholar, so he takes advantage of the popularity of the *Bhagavad-gītā* and writes a commentary. Such so-called scholars claim that anyone can give his own opinion. But in the *Bhagavad-gītā* Kṛṣṇa says that only His devotee can understand the *Gītā.* So these so-called scholars are cheating.

The conclusion is that if you want genuine spiritual knowledge you have to approach a bona fide spiritual master who has realized the Absolute Truth. Otherwise you will remain in darkness. You cannot think, "Oh, I may or may not accept a spiritual master. In any case, there are books that I can learn from." No, the Vedic injunction is *tad-vijñānārthaṁ sa gurum evābhigacchet.* The word gacchet means "one must go," not that one may or may not go. To understand transcendental knowledge, one must go to a spiritual master. That is the Vedic injunction.

You must know two things: what is *māyā* (illusion) and what is Kṛṣṇa. Then your knowledge is perfect. Of course, Kṛṣṇa is so nice that if you somehow or other fully surrender to Him, all your searching for knowledge will be finished: not only will you know what Kṛṣṇa is, but you will automatically learn what *māyā* is. Kṛṣṇa will give you intelligence from within.

So, by the mercy of both the spiritual master and Kṛṣṇa, one takes up devotional service. How is that? Their mercy runs on parallel lines. If you have not yet found a spiritual master but are sincere, Kṛṣṇa will direct you to a bona fide spiritual master. And if you get a bona fide spiritual master, he will take you to Kṛṣṇa. Kṛṣṇa is always sitting in your heart as the *caitya-guru,* the spiritual master within. It is that *caitya-guru* who manifests Himself externally as the spiritual master. Therefore the spiritual master is the direct representative of Kṛṣṇa.

The *Īśopaniṣad* says we should learn what vidyā and avidyā are. *Avidyā* is ignorance under the guise of materialistic knowledge. Śrīla Bhaktivinoda Ṭhākura writes in one of his songs that "advancement of material knowledge is simply the advancement of *māyā's* jurisdiction." The more you become implicated in material knowledge, the less you can understand Kṛṣṇa consciousness. Those who are advanced in material knowledge think, "What use is this Kṛṣṇa consciousness movement?" They have no attraction for spiritual knowledge; they are too absorbed in *avidyā.*

Some Indian boys reject the spiritual culture of India and come to the West to learn technology. When they see that I have introduced in the West the things they rejected in India, they are surprised. One reason I came to the West is that modern India has rejected spiritual knowledge. Today Indians think that if they can imitate Western technology, they will be happy. This is *māyā.* They do not see that those who are three hundred times more technologically advanced than the Indians are not happy. India will not be able to equal American or European technology for at least three hundred years because the Western countries have been developing technology for a very long time. But since the time of creation Indian culture has been a spiritual culture.

Vidyā, or genuine spiritual knowledge, does not depend on technology. Śrīla Vyāsadeva is the original *guru* of Vedic knowledge. How was he living? In a cottage in Baḍarikāśrama. But just see his knowledge! He wrote so many *Purāṇas,* including the *Śrīmad-Bhāgavatam.* He also wrote the *Vedānta-sūtra* and the *Mahābhārata.* If you studied every single verse written by Vyāsadeva, it would take your whole life. The *Śrīmad-Bhāgavatam* alone has no less than eighteen thousand verses. And each verse is so full of meaning that it would take a whole lifetime to fully understand it. This is Vedic culture.

There is no knowledge comparable to that contained in the Vedic literature—not only spiritual knowledge, but material knowledge also. The *Vedas* discuss astronomy, mathematics, and many other subjects. It is not that in ancient times there were no airplanes. They are mentioned in the *Purāṇas.* These airplanes were so strong and swift that they could easily reach other planets. It is not that there was no advancement of material knowledge in the Vedic age. It was there. But the people then did not consider it so important. They were interested in spiritual knowledge.

So, one should know what knowledge is, and what nescience is. If we advance in nescience, or material knowledge, we will have to undergo repeated birth and death. Moreover, there is no guarantee what your next birth will be. That is not in your hands. Now you are happy being an American, but after quitting this body you cannot dictate, "Please give me an American body again." Yes, you may get an American body, but it may be an American cow's body. Then you are destined for the slaughterhouse.

So, cultivating material knowledge—nationalism, socialism, this "ism," that "ism"—is simply a dangerous waste of time. Better to cultivate real knowledge, Vedic knowledge, which leads one to surrender to Kṛṣṇa. As Kṛṣṇa says in the *Bhagavad-gītā* (7.19), *bahūnāṁ janmanām ante jñānavān māṁ prapadyate.* After many, many births, one who is in genuine knowledge comes to Kṛṣṇa and surrenders to Him, realizing, "O Kṛṣṇa, You are everything." This is the culmination of all cultivation of knowledge.

Beyond the White Light of Brahman

The *Īśopaniṣad* states, "One should know perfectly the Personality of Godhead and His transcendental name, as well as the temporary material creation with its temporary demigods, men, and animals. When one knows these, he surpasses death and the ephemeral cosmic manifestation with it, and in the eternal kingdom of God he enjoys his eternal life of bliss and knowledge. O my Lord, sustainer of all that lives, Your real face is covered by Your dazzling effulgence. Kindly remove that covering and exhibit Yourself to Your pure devotee."

Here the *Īśopaniṣad* mentions the kingdom of God. Every planet, both spiritual and material, has a predominating deity. In the sun, for example, the predominating deity is Vivasvān. We get this information from the *Bhagavad-gītā.* So, there are millions and trillions of universes within the material sky, and within each universe are millions and trillions of planets, and in every planet there is a predominating deity.

Beyond the material sky is the *brahmajyoti,* or spiritual sky, where there are innumerable Vaikuṇṭha planets. Each Vaikuṇṭha planet is predominated by the Supreme Lord in His Nārāyaṇa form, and each Nārāyaṇa has a different name—Pradyumna, Ani-ruddha, Saṅkarṣaṇa, etc. One cannot see these planets because they are covered by the spiritual *brahmajyoti* effulgence, just as one cannot see the sun globe on account of the dazzling sunshine. The effulgence in the spiritual sky is coming out of Kṛṣṇa's planet, Goloka Vṛndāvana, which is above even Vaikuṇṭha. In Gokola Kṛṣṇa alone is the predominator.

The planet of the Absolute Truth, Kṛṣṇa, is covered by the Brahman effulgence. One has to penetrate that effulgence in order to see the Lord. Therefore in the *Īśopaniṣad* the devotee prays, "Kindly remove Your effulgence so I can see You." The Māyāvādī philosophers do not know that there is something beyond the *brahmajyoti.* But here in the *Īśopaniṣad* is the Vedic evidence that the *brahmajyoti* is simply a golden effulgence covering the real face of the Supreme Lord.

The idea is that Kṛṣṇa's planet and the Vaikuṇṭha planets are beyond the Brahman effulgence and that only devotees can enter those spiritual planets. The *jñānīs*, the mental speculators, practice severe austerities to enter the Brahman effulgence. But the demons who are killed by Kṛṣṇa are immediately transferred to that Brahman effulgence. So just consider: Is the place that is given to the enemies of Kṛṣṇa very covetable? If my enemy comes to my house, I may give him some place to stay, but if my intimate friend comes, I give him a much nicer place to stay. So this Brahman effulgence is not at all covetable.

Śrīla Prabodhānanda Sarasvatī has composed a nice verse in which he says that for the devotee, for one who has attained the mercy of the Lord, the Brahman effulgence is just like hell. Then what about heaven? The *karmīs,* or fruitive workers, are very eager to go to the heavenly planets, where the demigods reside. But for the devotees heaven is just a will-o'-the-wisp. They are not at all attracted to go there. And then there are the mystic *yogīs*, who try very strenuously to control the senses in order to attain special powers. The senses are like venomous serpents because as soon as you indulge in sense gratification—as soon as the senses "bite" you—you become degraded. But the devotee says, "I do not fear the poisonous serpents of the senses." Why? "Because I have extracted their fangs." In other words, by engaging his senses in Kṛṣṇa's service, the devotee is no longer tempted to indulge in sense gratification, and thus his senses cannot drag him down to a hellish condition of life.

In this way, the devotees are above the *karmīs, jñānīs*, and *yogīs*. The devotees' place is the highest because only by devotion can one understand God. Kṛṣṇa does not say you can understand Him by fruitive work. He does not say you can understand Him by speculation. He does not say you can understand Him by mystic yoga. He clearly says (Bg. 18.55), *bhaktyā mām abhi-jānāti yāvān yaś cāsmi tattvataḥ:* "Only by devotional service can one truly understand Me as I am."

Except for devotional service, there is no possibility of understanding the Absolute Truth. Any other process is imperfect because it is based on speculation. For example, the scientists may speculate on what the sun planet is, but because they have no access there, they cannot actually know what the sun planet is. They can only speculate. That's all. Once three blind men came upon an elephant. They began feeling the elephant and speculating on what it was. One felt its big legs and concluded, "Oh, the elephant is just like a pillar." The second man felt the trunk and concluded, "Oh, this elephant is just like a snake." And the third man felt the belly of the elephant and concluded, "This elephant is like a big boat." But actually, the blind men did not know what the elephant really was.

If you have no ability to see something, you can only speculate about it. Therefore the *Īśopaniṣad* says, "Please remove this brilliant effulgence covering Your face so I can see You." That seeing power is bestowed upon the devotee by Kṛṣṇa when He sees the devotee's love for Him. As the *Brahma-saṁhitā* says, *premāñjana-cchurita-bhakti-vilocanena*: The devotees anoint their eyes with the salve of love of God, and therefore they can see the Lord's beautiful form within their hearts. In India there is a special eye ointment. If you apply it you can immediately see clearly. Similarly, if you smear your eyes with the ointment of love of Godhead, you will see God always. This is the way of understanding God—by service and by enhancing your love for Him. This love can be developed only by devotional service; otherwise there is no possibility of achieving it. So the more you increase your spirit of service to God, the more you increase your dormant love for God. And as soon as you are in the perfectional stage of love of God, you will see God always, at every moment.

CHAPTER 2

BAD KARMA

The Śrīmad-Bhāgavatam is an ancient Sanskrit scripture that contains the essence of all Vedic wisdom, recording the teachings of the Lord's devotees, as well as those of the Lord in many of His incarnations. In this Thirtieth Chapter of the Third Canto, an incarnation of Kṛṣṇa's named Kapiladeva graphically describes the results of sin. Śrīla Prabhupāda explains the texts in his purports.

TEXT 1: The Personality of Godhead said, "As a mass of clouds does not know the powerful influence of the wind, a person engaged in material consciousness does not know the powerful strength of the time factor, by which he is being carried."

PURPORT: The great politician-*paṇḍita* named Cāṇakya said that even one moment of time cannot be returned, even if one is prepared to pay millions of dollars. One cannot calculate the amount of loss there is in wasting valuable time. Whether materially or spiritually, one should be very alert in utilizing the time which he has at his disposal. A conditioned soul lives in a particular body for a fixed measurement of time, and it is recommended in the scriptures that within that small measurement of time one has to finish Kṛṣṇa consciousness and thus gain release from the influence of the time factor. But, unfortunately, those who are not in Kṛṣṇa consciousness are carried away by the strong power of time without their knowledge, as clouds are carried by the wind.

TEXT 2: "Whatever is produced by the materialist with great pain and labor for so-called happiness, the Supreme Personality, as the time factor, destroys, and for this reason the conditioned soul laments."

PURPORT: The main function of the time factor, which is a representative of the Supreme Personality of Godhead, is to destroy everything. The materialists, in material consciousness, are engaged in producing so many things in the name of economic development. They think that by advancing in satisfying the material needs of man they will be happy, but they forget that everything they have produced will be destroyed in due course of time. From history we can see that there were many powerful empires on the surface of the globe that were constructed with great pain and great perseverance, but in due course of time they have all been destroyed. Still the foolish materialists cannot understand that they are simply wasting time in producing so-called material necessities, which are destined to be vanquished in due course of time. This waste of energy is due to the ignorance of the mass of people, who do not know that they are eternal and that they have an eternal engagement also. They do not know that this span of life in a particular type of body is but a flash in the eternal journey. Not knowing this fact, they take the small flash of their present life to be everything, and they waste time in improving economic conditions.

TEXT 3: "The misguided materialist does not know that his very body is impermanent and that the attractions of home, land, and wealth, which are in relationship to that body, are also temporary. Out of ignorance only, he thinks that everything is permanent."

PURPORT: The materialist thinks that persons engaged in Kṛṣṇa consciousness are crazy fellows wasting time by chanting Hare Kṛṣṇa, but actually he does not know that he himself is in the darkest region of craziness because of accepting his body as permanent. And in relation to his body he accepts his home, his country, his society, and all other paraphernalia as permanent. This materialistic acceptance of the permanence of home, land, etc. is called the illusion of *māyā*. This is clearly mentioned here. *Mohād gṛha-kṣetra-vasūni*: out of illusion only does the materialist accept his home, his land, and his money as permanent. Out of this illusion have grown family life, national life, and economic development, which are very important factors in modern civilization. A Kṛṣṇa conscious person knows that this economic development of human society is but temporary illusion.

In another part of the *Śrīmad-Bhāgavatam*, the acceptance of the body as oneself, the acceptance of others as kinsmen in relationship to one's body, and the acceptance of the land of one's birth as worshipable are declared to be the products of an animal civilization. When, however, one is enlightened in Kṛṣṇa consciousness, one can use these for the service of the Lord. That is a very suitable proposition. Everything has a relationship with Kṛṣṇa. When all economic development and material advancement are utilized to advance the cause of Kṛṣṇa consciousness, a new phase of progressive life arises.

TEXT 4: "In whatever species of life the living entity appears, he finds a particular type of satisfaction in that species, and he is never averse to being situated in such a condition."

PURPORT: The satisfaction of the living entity in a particular type of body, even if it is most abominable, is called illusion. A man in a higher position may feel dissatisfaction with the standard of life of a lower-grade man, but the lower-grade man is satisfied in that position because of the spell of *māyā*, the external energy. *Māyā* has two phases of activity. One is called *prakṣepātmikā,* and the other is called *āvaraṇātmikā*. *Āvaraṇātmikā* means "covering," and *prakṣepātmikā* means "pulling down." In any condition of life, the materialistic person or animal will be satisfied because his knowledge is covered by the influence of *māyā*. In the lower grade or lower species of life, the development of consciousness is so poor that one cannot understand whether one is happy or distressed. This is *called āvaraṇātmikā*. Even a hog, who lives by eating stool, thinks himself happy, although a person in a higher mode of life sees how abominable that life is.

TEXT 5: "While deluded by the covering influence of the illusory energy, the living entity feels little inclined to cast off his body, even when in hell, for he takes delight in hellish enjoyment."

PURPORT: It is said that once Indra, the king of heaven, was cursed by his spiritual master, Bṛhaspati, on account of his misbehavior, and he became a hog on this planet. After many days, when Brahmā wanted to recall him to his heavenly kingdom, Indra, in the form of a hog, forgot everything of his royal position in the heavenly kingdom, and he refused to go back. This is the spell of *māyā*. Even Indra forgets his heavenly standard of life and is satisfied with the standard of a hog's life.

By the influence of *māyā* the conditioned soul becomes so affectionate toward his particular type of body that even if someone says to him, “Give up this body, and immediately you will have a king's body,” he will not agree. This attachment strongly affects all conditioned living entities. Lord Kṛṣṇa personally canvasses, “Give up everything in this material world. Come to Me, and I shall give you all protection,” but we are not agreeable. We think, “We are quite all right. Why should we surrender unto Kṛṣṇa and go back to His kingdom?” This is called illusion, or *māyā*. Everyone is satisfied with his standard of living, however abominable it may be.

TEXT 6: “Such satisfaction with one's standard of living is due to deep-rooted attraction for body, wife, home, children, animals, wealth, and friends. In such association, the conditioned soul thinks himself quite perfect.”

PURPORT: This so-called perfection of human life is a concoction. Therefore it is said that however materially qualified a person may be, if he is not a devotee of the Lord he has no good qualities because he is hovering on the mental plane, which will drag him again to the material existence of temporary life. One who acts on the mental plane cannot get promotion to the spiritual plane. Such a person is always sure to glide down again to material life. Still, in the association of so-called society, friendship, and love, the conditioned soul feels completely satisfied.

TEXT 7: “Although he is always burning with anxiety, such a fool always performs all kinds of mischievous activities with the unfulfillable hope of maintaining his so-called family and society.”

PURPORT: It is said that it is easier to maintain a great empire than a small family, especially in these days, when the influence of Kali-yuga is so strong that everyone is harassed and full of anxieties because of accepting the false presentation of *māyā's* family. The family we maintain is created by *māyā;* it is the perverted reflection of the family in Kṛṣṇaloka. In Kṛṣṇaloka there are also family, friends, society, father, and mother; everything is there, but they are eternal. Here, as we change bodies our family relationships also change. Sometimes we are in a family of human beings, sometimes in a family of demigods, sometimes a family of cats or dogs.

Family, society, and friendship are flickering, and so they are called *asat*. It is said that as long as we are attached to this *asat*—this temporary, nonexistent society and family—we are always full of anxieties. The materialists do not know that the family, society, and friendship here in this material world are only shadows, and thus they become attached. Naturally their hearts are always burning, but in spite of all inconvenience, they still work to maintain such false families because they have no information of the real family association with Kṛṣṇa.

TEXT 8: "He gives heart and senses to a woman, who falsely charms him with *māyā*. He enjoys solitary embraces and talking with her, and he is enchanted by the sweet words of the small children."

PURPORT: Family life within the kingdom of the illusory energy, *māyā,* is just like a prison for the eternal living entity. In prison a prisoner is shackled by iron chains and iron bars. Similarly, a conditioned soul is shackled by the charming beauty of a woman, by her solitary embraces and talks of so-called love, and by the sweet words of his small children. Thus he forgets his real identity.

In this verse the words *strīṇām asatīnām* indicate that womanly love exists just to agitate the mind of man. Actually, in the material world there is no love. Both the woman and the man are interested in their sense gratification. For sense gratification a woman creates an illusory love, and the man becomes enchanted by such false love and forgets his real duty. When there are children as the result of such a combination, the next attraction is to the sweet words of the children. The love of the woman at home and the talk of the children make one a secure prisoner, and thus he cannot leave his home. Such a person is termed, in Vedic language, a *gṛhamedhī,* which means "one whose center of attraction is home." The word *gṛhastha* refers to one who lives with family, wife, and children but whose real purpose of living is to develop Kṛṣṇa consciousness. One is therefore advised to become a *gṛhastha,* not a *gṛhamedhī.* The *gṛhastha's* concern is to get out of the family life created by illusion and enter into real family life with Kṛṣṇa, whereas the *gṛhamedhī's* business is to repeatedly chain himself to so-called family life, in one life after another, and perpetually remain in the darkness of *māyā.*

TEXT 9: "The attached householder remains in his family life, which is full of diplomacy and politics. Always spreading miseries and controlled by acts of sense gratification, he acts just to counteract the reactions of all his miseries, and if he can successfully counteract such miseries, he thinks he is happy."

PURPORT: In the *Bhagavad-gītā* the Personality of Godhead Himself certifies the material world as an impermanent place that is full of miseries. There is no question of happiness in this material world, either individually or in terms of family, society, or country. If something is going on in the name of happiness, that is illusion. Here in this material world, happiness means successful counteraction of distress. The material world is so made that unless one becomes a clever diplomat, his life will be a failure. What to speak of human society, even in the society of lower animals, the birds and beasts cleverly manage their bodily demands of eating, sleeping, mating, and defending. Human society competes nationally or individually, and in the attempt to be successful the entire human society becomes full of diplomacy. We should always remember that in spite of all diplomacy and all intelligence in the struggle for existence, everything will end in a second by the supreme will. Therefore, all our attempts to become happy in this material world are simply a delusion offered by *māyā.*

TEXT 10: "He secures money by committing violence here and there, and although he employs it in the service of his family, he himself eats only a little portion of the food thus purchased, and he goes to hell for those for whom he earned the money in such an irregular way."

PURPORT: There is a Bengali proverb: "The person for whom I have stolen accuses me of being a thief." The family members for whom an attached person acts in so many criminal ways are never satisfied. In illusion an attached person serves such family members, and by serving them he is destined to enter into a hellish condition of life. For example, a thief steals something to maintain his family, and he is caught and imprisoned. This is the sum and substance of material existence and attachment to material society, friendship, and love. Although an attached family man is always engaged in getting money by hook or by crook for the maintenance of his family, he cannot enjoy more than what he could consume even without such criminal activities. A man who eats eight ounces of food may have to maintain a big family and earn money by any means to support that family, but he himself is not offered more than what he can eat, and sometimes he eats the remnants that are left after his family members are fed. Even by earning money by unfair means, he cannot enjoy life for himself. That is called the covering illusion of *māyā*.

The process of illusory service to society, country, and community is exactly the same everywhere; the same principle is applicable even to big national leaders. A national leader who is very great in serving his country is sometimes killed by his countrymen because of irregular service. In other words, one cannot satisfy his dependents by this illusory service, although one cannot get out of the service because being a servant is his constitutional position.

A living entity is constitutionally part and parcel of the Supreme Being, but he forgets that he has to render service to the Supreme Being and diverts his attention to serving others; this is called *māyā*. By serving others he falsely thinks that he is master. The head of a family thinks of himself as the master of the family, or the leader of a nation thinks of himself as the master of the nation, whereas actually he is serving, and by serving *māyā* he is gradually going to hell. Therefore a sane man should come to the point of Kṛṣṇa consciousness and engage in the service of the Supreme Lord, applying his whole life, all of his wealth, his entire intelligence, and his full power of speaking.

TEXTS 11-13: "When he suffers reverses in his occupation, he tries again and again to improve himself, but when he is baffled in all attempts and is ruined, he accepts money from others because of excessive greed. Thus the unfortunate man, unsuccessful in maintaining his family members, is bereft of all beauty. He always thinks of his failure, grieving very deeply. Seeing him unable to support them, his wife and others do not treat him with the same respect as before, even as miserly farmers do not accord the same treatment to their old and worn-out oxen."

PURPORT: Not only in the present age but from time immemorial no one has liked an old man who is unable to earn in the family. Even in the modern age, in some communities or states, the old men are given poison so that they will die as soon as possible. In some cannibalistic communities, the old grandfather is sportingly killed, and a feast is held in which his body is eaten. Here the example is given that a farmer does not like an old ox who has ceased to work. Similarly, when an attached person in family life becomes old and is unable to earn, he is no longer liked by his wife, sons, daughters, and other kinsmen, and he is consequently neglected, what to speak of not being given respect. It is judicious, therefore, to give up family attachment before one attains old age and take shelter of the Supreme Personality of Godhead. A person should employ himself in the Lord's service so that the Supreme Lord can take charge of him and he will not be neglected by his so-called kinsmen.

TEXT 14: "The foolish family man does not become averse to family life although he is maintained by those whom he once maintained. Deformed by the influence of old age, he prepares himself to meet ultimate death."

PURPORT: Family attraction is so strong that even if a person is neglected by family members in his old age, he cannot give up family affection, and he remains at home just like a dog. In the Vedic way of life, it is advised that before getting too weak and being baffled in material activities, and before becoming diseased, one should give up family life and engage oneself completely in the service of the Lord for the remaining days of his life.

Therefore the Vedic scriptures enjoin that as soon as one passes fifty years of age, he must give up family life and live alone in the forest. After preparing himself fully, he should become a *sannyāsī*, travel widely, and distribute the knowledge of spiritual life to each and every home.

TEXT 15: "Thus he remains at home just like a pet dog and eats whatever is so negligently given to him. Afflicted with many illnesses, such as dyspepsia and loss of appetite, he eats only very small morsels of food, and he becomes an invalid, who cannot work any more."

PURPORT: Before meeting death a man is sure to become a diseased invalid, and when he is neglected by his family members, his life becomes less than a dog's because he is put into so many miserable conditions. Vedic literatures enjoin, therefore, that before the arrival of such miserable conditions, a man should leave home and die without the knowledge of his family members. If a man leaves home and dies without his family's knowing, that is considered a glorious death. But an attached family man wants his family members to carry him in a great procession even after his death, and although he will not be able to see how the procession goes, he still desires that his body be taken gorgeously in procession. Thus he is happy without even knowing where he has to go when he leaves his body for the next life.

TEXTS 16-17: "In that diseased condition, a man's eyes bulge due to the pressure of air from within, and his glands become congested with mucus. He has difficulty breathing, and upon exhaling and inhaling he produces a sound like *ghura-ghura,* a rattling within the throat. In this way he comes under the clutches of death and lies down, surrounded by lamenting friends and relatives, and although he wants to speak with them, he no longer can because he is under the control of time."

PURPORT: For formality's sake, when a man is lying on his deathbed, his relatives come to him, and sometimes they cry very loudly, addressing the dying man: "O my father!" "O my friend!" or "O my husband!" In that pitiable condition the dying man wants to speak with them and instruct them of his desires, but because he is fully under the control of the time factor, death, he cannot express himself, and that causes him in-conceivable pain. He is already in a painful condition because of disease, and his glands and throat are choked up with mucus. He is already in a very difficult position, and when he is addressed by his relatives in that way, his grief increases.

TEXT 18: "Thus the man who engaged with uncontrolled senses in maintaining his family dies in great grief, seeing his relatives crying. He dies most pathetically, in great pain and without consciousness."

PURPORT: In the *Bhagavad-gītā* it is said that at the time of death one will be absorbed in the thoughts he cultivated during his lifetime. A person who had no idea other than to properly maintain his family members must have family affairs in his last thoughts. That is the natural sequence for a common man. The common man does not know the destiny of his life; he is simply busy in this present flash of life, maintaining his family. At the last stage, no one is satisfied with how he has improved the family economic condition; everyone thinks that he could not provide sufficiently. Because of his deep family affection, he forgets his main duty of controlling his senses and improving his spiritual consciousness. Sometimes a dying man entrusts the family affairs to either his son or some relative, saying, "I am going. Please look after the family." He does not know where he is going, but even at the time of death he is anxious about how his family will be maintained. Sometimes it is seen that a dying man requests the physician to increase his life at least for a few years so that the family maintenance plan which he has begun can be completed. These are the material diseases of the conditioned soul. He completely forgets his real engagement—to become Kṛṣṇa conscious—and is always serious about planning to maintain his family, although he changes families one after another.

TEXT 19: "At death, he sees the messengers of the lord of death come before him, their eyes full of wrath, and in great fear he passes stool and urine."

PURPORT: There are two kinds of transmigration of a living entity after passing away from the present body. One kind of transmigration is to go to the controller of sinful activities, who is known as Yamarāja, and the other is to go to the higher planets, up to Vaikuṇṭha. Here Lord Kapila describes how persons engaged in activities of sense gratification to maintain a family are treated by the messengers of Yamarāja, called Yamadūtas. At the time of death the Yamadūtas become the custodians of those persons who have strongly gratified their senses. They take charge of the dying man and take him to the planet where Yamarāja resides. The conditions there are described in the following verses.

TEXT 20: "As a criminal is arrested for punishment by the constables of the state, a person engaged in criminal sense gratification is similarly arrested by the Yamadūtas, who bind him by the neck with strong rope and cover his subtle body so that he may undergo severe punishment."

PURPORT: Every living entity is covered by a subtle body and a gross body. The subtle body is the covering of mind, ego, intelligence, and consciousness. It is said in the scriptures that the constables of Yamarāja cover the subtle body of the culprit and take him to the abode of Yamarāja to be punished in a way that he is able to tolerate. He does not die from this punishment because if he died, then who would suffer the punishment? It is not the business of the constables of Yamarāja to put one to death. In fact, it is not possible to kill a living entity because factually he is eternal; he simply has to suffer the consequences of his activities of sense gratification.

The process of punishment is explained in the *Caitanya-caritāmṛta.* Formerly the king's men would take a criminal in a boat in the middle of the river. They would dunk him by grasping a bunch of his hair and thrusting him completely under water, and when he was almost suffocated, the king's constables would take him out of the water and allow him to breathe for some time, and then they would again dunk him in the water to suffocate. This sort of punishment is inflicted upon the forgotten soul by Yamarāja, as will be described in the following verses.

TEXT 21: While carried by the constables of Yamarāja, he is overwhelmed and trembles in their hands. While passing on the road he is bitten by dogs, and he can remember the sinful activities of his life. He is thus terribly distressed."

PURPORT: It appears from this verse that while passing from this planet to the planet of Yamarāja, the culprit arrested by Yamarāja's constables meets many dogs, which bark and bite just to remind him of his criminal activities of sense gratification. It is said in the *Bhagavad-gītā* that one becomes almost blind and is bereft of all sense when he is infuriated by the desire for sense gratification. He forgets everything. A man is bereft of all intelligence when he is too attracted by sense gratification, and he forgets that he has to suffer the consequences also. Here the chance for recounting his activities of sense gratification is given by the dogs engaged by Yamarāja. While we live in the gross body, such activities of sense gratification are encouraged, even by modern governments. In many states all over the world, the government encourages such activities by pushing birth control. Women are supplied pills, and they are allowed to go to a clinical laboratory to get assistance for abortions. This is going on as a result of sense gratification. Actually sex is meant for begetting a good child, but because people have no control over the senses and there is no institution to train them to control the senses, the poor people fall victim to the criminal offenses of sense gratification, and they are punished after death as described in these passages of the *Śrīmad-Bhāgavatam*.

TEXTS 22-24: "Under the scorching sun, the criminal has to pass through roads of hot sand with forest fires on both sides. He is whipped on the back by the constables because of his inability to walk, and he is afflicted by hunger and thirst. But unfortunately there is no drinking water, no shelter, and no place for rest on the road. While passing on that road to the abode of Yamarāja, he falls down in fatigue, and sometimes he becomes unconscious, but he is forced to rise again.

"In this way he is very quickly brought to the presence of Yamarāja. Thus he has to pass ninety-nine thousand *yojanas* within two or three moments, and then he is at once engaged in the torturous punishment he is destined to suffer."

PURPORT: One *yojana* is eight miles, and thus he has to pass along a road that is as much as 792,000 miles long. Such a long distance is passed over within a few moments only. The subtle body is covered by the constables so that the living entity can travel such a long distance quickly and at the same time tolerate the suffering. This covering, although material, is of such fine elements that material scientists cannot discover what the coverings are made of. To pass 792,000 miles within a few moments seems wonderful to the modern space travelers. They have so far traveled at a speed of 18,000 miles per hour, but here we see that a criminal passes 792,000 miles within a few seconds only, although the process is not spiritual but material.

TEXT 25: "He is placed in the midst of burning pieces of wood, and his limbs are set on fire. In some cases he is made to eat his own flesh or have it eaten by others."

PURPORT: This verse and the next three verses describe the sinful living entity's punishment. The first description is that the criminal has to eat his own flesh, burning with fire, or allow others like himself who are present there to eat it. In the last great war, people in concentration camps sometimes ate their own stool, so there is no wonder that in Yamasādana, the abode of Yamarāja, a meat-eater who had a very enjoyable life eating others' flesh has to eat his own flesh.

TEXTS 26-28: "His entrails are pulled out by the hounds and vultures of hell, even though he is still alive to see it, and he is subjected to torment by serpents, scorpions, gnats, and other creatures that bite him. Next his limbs are lopped off and torn asunder by elephants. He is hurled down from hilltops, and he is also held captive either in water or in a cave.

"Men and women whose lives were built upon indulgence in illicit sex are put into many kinds of miserable conditions in the hells known as Tāmisra, Andha-tāmisra, and Raurava."

PURPORT: The lives of all materialistic people, who are undergoing severe tribulation in the struggle for existence, are based on sex. Therefore, in the Vedic civilization sex is allowed only in a restricted way; it is for the married couple, and only for begetting children. But when sex is indulged in for sense gratification illegally and illicitly, both the man and the woman await severe punishment in this world or after death. In this world they are punished by virulent diseases like syphilis and gonorrhea, and in the next life, as we see in this passage of the *Śrīmad-Bhāgavatam*, they are put into various kinds of hellish conditions to suffer.

In the *Bhagavad-gītā,* First Chapter, illicit sex is also very much condemned, and it is said that one who produces children by illicit sex is sent to hell. It is confirmed here in the *Bhāgavatam* that such offenders are put into hellish conditions of life in Tāmisra, Andhatāmisra, and Raurava.

TEXT 29: Lord Kapila continued, "My dear mother, it is sometimes said that we experience hell or heaven on this planet, for hellish punishments are sometimes visible on this planet also."

PURPORT: Sometimes unbelievers do not accept these statements of scripture regarding hell. Lord Kapila therefore confirms them by saying that these hellish conditions are also visible on this planet. It is not that they are only on the planet where Yamarāja lives. On the planet of Yamarāja, the sinful man is given the chance to practice living in the hellish conditions that he will have to endure in the next life, and then he is given a chance to take birth on another planet to continue his hellish life.

For example, if a man is to be punished to remain in hell and eat stool and urine, then first of all he practices such habits on the planet of Yamarāja, and then he is given a particular type of body, that of a hog, so that he can eat stool and think he is enjoying life. It is stated previously that in any hellish condition, the conditioned soul thinks he is happy. Otherwise, it would not be possible for him to suffer hellish life.

TEXT 30: "After leaving this body, the man who maintained himself and his family members by sinful activities suffers a hellish life, and his relatives suffer also."

PURPORT: The mistake of modern civilization is that man does not believe in the next life. But whether he believes or not, the next life is there, and one has to suffer if one does not lead a responsible life in terms of the injunctions of authoritative scriptures like the *Vedas* and *Purāṇas.* Species lower than human beings are not responsible for their actions because they are made to act in a certain way, but in the developed life of human consciousness, one who does not act responsibly is sure to get a hellish life, as described herein.

TEXT 31: "He goes alone to the darkest regions of hell after quitting the present body, and the money he acquired by envying other living entities is the passage money with which he leaves this world."

PURPORT: When a man earns money by unfair means and maintains his family and himself with that money, the money is enjoyed by many members of the family, but he alone goes to hell and suffers the resultant sinful reactions accrued from such a violent and illicit life. For example, if a man secures some money by killing someone and with that money maintains his family, those who enjoy the black money earned by him are also partially responsible and are also sent to hell, but he who is the leader is especially punished. The money he earned is left in this world, and he takes only the sinful reaction.

In this world also, if a person acquires some money by murdering someone, the family is not hanged, although its members are sinfully contaminated. But the man who commits the murder and maintains his family is himself hanged as a murderer. The direct offender is more responsible for sinful activities than the indirect enjoyer. The great learned scholar Cāṇakya Paṇḍita says, therefore, that whatever one has in his possession had better be spent for the cause of sat, or the Supreme Personality of Godhead, because one cannot take his possessions with him. They remain here, and they will be lost. Either we leave the money or the money leaves us, but we will be separated. The best use of money as long as it is within our possession is to spend it to acquire and propagate Kṛṣṇa consciousness.

TEXT 32: "Thus, by the arrangement of the Supreme Personality of Godhead, the maintainer of kinsmen is put into a hellish condition to suffer for his sinful activities, like a man who has lost his wealth."

PURPORT: The example set herein is that the sinful person suffers just like a man who has lost his wealth. The human form of body is achieved by the conditioned soul after many, many births and is a very valuable asset. Instead of utilizing this life to get liberation, if one uses it simply for the purpose of maintaining his so-called family and therefore performs foolish and unauthorized action, he is compared to a man who has lost his wealth and who, upon losing it, laments. When wealth is lost, there is no use lamenting, but as long as there is wealth, one has to utilize it properly and thereby gain eternal profit. It may be argued that when a man leaves his money earned by sinful activities, he also leaves his sinful activities here with his money. But it is especially mentioned herein that by superior arrangement, although the man leaves behind his sinfully earned money, he carries the effect of it.

When a man steals some money, if he is caught and agrees to return it, he is not freed from the criminal punishment. By the law of the state, even though he returns the money, he has to undergo the punishment. Similarly, the money earned by a criminal process may be left by the man when dying, but by superior arrangement he carries with him the effect, and therefore he has to suffer hellish life.

TEXT 33: "Therefore a person who is very eager to maintain his family and kinsmen simply by black methods certainly goes to the darkest region of hell, which is known as Andha-tāmisra."

PURPORT: Three words in this verse are very significant. *Kevalena* means "only by black methods," *adharmeṇa* means "unrighteous" or "irreligious," and *kuṭumba-bharaṇa* means "family maintenance." Maintaining one's family is certainly the duty of a householder, but one should be eager to earn his livelihood by the prescribed method, as stated in the scriptures. In the *Bhagavad-gītā* it is described that the Lord has divided the social system into four classifications of castes, or *varṇas*, according to quality and work. Apart from the *Bhagavad-gītā*, in every society a man is known according to his quality and work. For example, when a man earns his livelihood constructing wooden furniture, he is called a carpenter, and a man who works with an anvil and iron is called a blacksmith. Similarly, a man who is engaged in the medical or engineering fields has a particular duty and designation. All these human activities have been divided by the Supreme Lord into four *varṇas,* namely the *brāhmaṇas* (intellectuals and priests), the *kṣatriyas* (warriors and administrators), the *vaiśyas* (merchants and farmers), and *śūdras* (manual laborers). In the *Bhagavad-gītā* and other Vedic scriptures, the specific duties of the *brāhmaṇas*, *kṣatriyas*, *vaiśyas,* and *śūdras* are mentioned.

One should work honestly according to his qualification. He should not earn his livelihood unfairly or in a way for which he is not qualified. If someone claims to be a *brāhmaṇa* and works as a priest, attracting people who expect to be enlightened about the spiritual way of life, but he is not qualified as a priest, then he is cheating the public. One should not earn one's livelihood by such unfair means. The same is applicable to a *kṣatriya* and a *vaiśya.* It is especially mentioned that the means of livelihood of those who are trying to advance in Kṛṣṇa consciousness must be very fair and uncomplicated. Here it is mentioned that he who earns his livelihood by unfair means (*kevalena*) is sent to the darkest hellish region. Otherwise, if one maintains his family by prescribed methods and honest means, there is no objection to one's being a family man.

TEXT 34: "Having gone through all the miserable, hellish conditions and having passed in a regular order through the lowest forms of animal life prior to human birth, and having thus been purged of one's sins, one is reborn again as a human being on this earth."

PURPORT: Just as a prisoner who has undergone troublesome prison life is set free again, the person who has always engaged in impious and mischievous activities is put into hellish conditions, and when he has undergone different hellish lives, namely those of lower animals like cats, dogs, and hogs, by the gradual process of evolution he again comes back as a human being. In the *Bhagavad-gītā* it is stated that even though a person engaged in the practice of the yoga system may not finish perfectly and may fall down for some reason or other, his next life as a human being is guaranteed. It is stated that such a person, who has fallen from the path of *yoga* practice, is given a chance in his next life to take birth in a very rich family or in a very pious family. It is interpreted that "rich family" refers to a big mercantile family because generally people who engage in business are very rich. One who engaged in the process of self-realization, or connecting with the Supreme Absolute Truth, but fell short is allowed to take birth in such a rich family, or he is allowed to take birth in the family of pious *brāhmaṇas;* either way, he is guaranteed to appear in human society in his next life.

It can be concluded that if someone is not willing to enter into hellish life, as in Tāmisra or Andha-tāmisra, then he must take to the process of Kṛṣṇa consciousness, which is the first-class *yoga* system, because even if one is unable to attain complete Kṛṣṇa consciousness in this life, he is guaranteed at least to take his next birth in a human family. He cannot be sent into a hellish condition. Kṛṣṇa consciousness is the purest life, and it protects all human beings from gliding down to hell to take birth in a family of dogs or hogs.

CHAPTER 3

THE PEACE FORMULA

The laws of nature work collectively, as well as individually. In the following brief but cogent statement, Śrīla Prabhupāda explains that if we want to break out of the tangled web of collective karma that is wreaking havoc in present—day society—if we want peace both collectively and individually—we need to take to Kṛṣṇa consciousness seriously.

The great mistake of modern civilization is to encroach upon others' property as though it were one's own and thereby create an unnecessary disturbance of the laws of nature. These laws are very strong. No living entity can violate them. Only one who is Kṛṣṇa conscious can easily overcome the stringent laws of nature and thus become happy and peaceful in the world.

As a state is protected by the department of law and order, so the state of the universe, of which this earth is only an insignificant fragment, is protected by the laws of nature. This material nature is one of the different potencies of God, who is the ultimate proprietor of everything that be. This earth is, therefore, the property of God, but we, the living entities, especially the so-called civilized human beings, are claiming God's property as our own under both an individual and collective false conception. If you want peace, you have to remove this false conception from your mind and from the world. This false claim of proprietorship by the human race on earth is partly or wholly the cause of all disturbances of peace on earth.

Foolish so-called civilized men are claiming proprietary rights on the property of God because they have now become godless. You cannot be happy and peaceful in a godless society. In the *Bhagavad-gītā* Lord Kṛṣṇa says that He is the factual enjoyer of all activities of the living entities, that He is the Supreme Lord of all universes, and that He is the well-wishing friend of all beings. When the people of the world know this as the formula for peace, it is then and there that peace will prevail.

Therefore, if you want peace at all, you will have to change your consciousness into Kṛṣṇa consciousness, both individually and collectively, by the simple process of chanting the holy name of God. This is the standard and recognized process for achieving peace in the world. We therefore recommend that everyone become Kṛṣṇa conscious by chanting Hare Kṛṣṇa, Hare Kṛṣṇa, Kṛṣṇa Kṛṣṇa, Hare Hare/ Hare Rāma, Hare Rāma, Rāma Rāma, Hare Hare.

This is practical, simple, and sublime. Five hundred years ago this formula was introduced in India by Lord Śrī Caitanya, and now it is available throughout the world. Take to this simple process of chanting as above mentioned, realize your factual position by reading the *Bhagavad-gītā As It Is,* and reestablish your lost relationship with Kṛṣṇa, God. Peace and prosperity will be the immediate worldwide result.

About the Author

His Divine Grace A.C. Bhaktivedanta Swami Prabhupāda appeared in this world in 1896 in Calcutta, India. He first met his spiritual master, Śrīla Bhaktisiddhānta Sarasvatī Gosvāmi, in Calcutta in 1922. Śrīla Bhaktisiddhānta Sarasvatī, a prominent religious scholar and the founder of sixty-four Gauḍīya Maṭhas (Vedic institutes) in India, liked this educated young man and convinced him to dedicate his life to teaching Vedic knowledge. Śrīla Prabhupāda became his student and, in 1933, his formally initiated disciple.

At their first meeting, Śrīla Bhaktisiddhānta Sarasvatī requested Śrīla Prabhupāda to broadcast Vedic knowledge in English. In the years that followed, Śrīla Prabhupāda wrote a commentary on the *Bhagavad-gītā,* assisted the Gauḍīya Maṭha in its work, and, in 1944, started *Back to Godhead,* an English fortnightly magazine. Single-handedly, Śrīla Prabhupāda edited it, typed the manuscripts, checked the galley proofs, and even distributed the individual copies. The magazine is now being continued by his disciples all over the world.

In 1950 Śrīla Prabhupāda retired from married life, adopting the *vānaprastha* (retired) order to devote more time to his studies and writing. He traveled to the holy city of Vṛndāvana, where he lived in humble circumstances in the historic temple of Rādhā-Dāmodara. There he engaged for several years in deep study and writing. He accepted the renounced order of life (*sannyāsa*) in 1959. At Rādhā-Dāmodara, Śrīla Prabhupāda began work on his life's masterpiece: a multivolume commentated translation of the eighteen-thousand-verse *Śrīmad-Bhāgavatam* (*Bhāgavata Purāṇa*). He also wrote *Easy Journey to Other Planets.*

After publishing three volumes of the *Bhāgavatam,* Śrīla Prabhupāda came to the United States, in September 1965, to fulfill the mission of his spiritual master. Subsequently, His Divine Grace wrote more than fifty volumes of authoritative commentated translations and summary studies of the philosophical and religious classics of India.

When he first arrived by freighter in New York City, Śrīla Prabhupāda was practically penniless. It was after almost a year of great difficulty that he established the International Society for Krishna Consciousness in July of 1966. Before he passed away on November 14, 1977, he had guided the Society and seen it grow to a worldwide confederation of more than one hundred *ashrams,* schools, temples, institutes, and farm communities.

In 1972 His Divine Grace introduced the Vedic system of primary and secondary education in the West by founding the *gurukula* school in Dallas, Texas. Since then his disciples have established similar schools throughout the United States and the rest of the world.

Śrīla Prabhupāda also inspired the construction of several large international cultural centers in India. The center at Śrīdhāma Māyāpur is the site for a planned spiritual city, an ambitious project for which construction will extend over many years to come. In Vṛndāvana are the magnificent Kṛṣṇa-Balarāma Temple and International Guesthouse, *gurukula* school, and Śrīla Prabhupāda Memorial and Museum. There is also a major cultural and educational center in Mumbai. There are beautiful temples in Delhi, Bangalore, Ahmedabad and Vadodara besides many other centers throughout India.

Śrīla Prabhupāda's most significant contribution, however, is his books. Highly respected by scholars for their authority, depth, and clarity, they are used as textbooks in numerous college courses. His writings have been translated into over fifty languages. The Bhaktivedanta Book Trust, established in 1972 exclusively to publish the works of His Divine Grace, has thus become the world's largest publisher of books in the field of Indian religion and philosophy.

In just twelve years, despite his advanced age, Śrīla Prabhupāda circled the globe fourteen times on lecture tours that took him to six continents. In spite of such a vigorous schedule, Śrīla Prabhupāda continued to write prolifically. His writings constitute a veritable library of Vedic philosophy, religion, literature, and culture.

Sanskrit Pronunciation Guide

The system of transliteration used in this book conforms to a system that scholars have accepted to indicate the pronunciation of each sound in the Sanskrit language.

The short vowel **a** is pronounced like the **u** in but, long **ā** like the **a** in far. Short **i** is pronounced as in pin, long **ī** as in pique, short **u** as in pull, and long **ū** as in rule. The vowel **ṛ** is pronounced like the **ri** in rim, e like the ey in they, ***o*** like the ***o*** in **go, ai** like the **ai** in-aisle, and au like the **ow** in **how.** The *anusvāra* **(ṁ)** is pronounced like the n in the French word *bo***n**, and *visarga* (ḥ) is pronounced as a final **h** sound. At the end of a couplet, **aḥ** is pronounced **aha,** and **iḥ** is pronounced **ihi.**

The guttural consonants--**k, kh,** g, **gh**, and **ṅ--**are pronounced from the throat in much the same manner as in English. **K** is pronounced as in **k**ite, **kh** as in Ec**kh**art, **g** as in **g**ive, **gh** as in di**g h**ard, and **ṅ** as in si**ng**.

The palatal consonants--**c, ch, j, jh**, and **ñ--**are pronounced with the tongue touching the firm ridge behind the teeth. C is pronounced as in **ch**air, **ch** as in staun**ch-h**eart, **j** as in **j**oy, **jh** as in he**dgeh**og, and **ñ** as in ca**ny**on.

The cerebral consonants—**ṭ, ṭh, ḍ, ḍh**, and **ṇ--**are pronounced with the tip of the tongue turned up and drawn back against the dome of the palate. **Ṭ** is pronounced as in **t**ub, **ṭh** as in ligh**t-h**eart, **ḍ** as in **d**ove, **ḍh** as in re**d-h**ot and **ṇ** as in **n**ut. The dental consonants--**t, th, d, dh**, and **n**--are pronounced in the same manner as the cerebrals, but with the forepart of the tongue against the teeth.

The labial consonants--**p, ph, b, bh,** and **m**--are pronounced with the lips. **P** is pronounced as in **p**ine, **ph** as in u**ph**ill, **b** as in bird, **bh** as in ru**b-h**ard, and **m** as in **m**other.

The semivowels--**y, r, l,** and **v--**are pronounced as in **y**es, **r**un, **l**ight, and **v**ine respectively. The sibilants--**ś, s,** and **s**--are pronounced, respectively, as in the German word *sprechen* and the English words **sh**ine and sun. The letter **h** is pronounced as in **h**ome.

GLOSSARY

A

Ācārya—an ideal teacher, who teaches by his personal example; a spiritual master.

B

Badarikāśrama—a sacred place of pilgrimage in the Himālayas.

Bhagavad-gītā—the discourse between the Supreme Lord, Kṛṣṇa, and His devotee Arjuna expounding devotional service as both the principal means and the ultimate end of spiritual perfection.

Bhaktivinoda Ṭhākura (1838-1915)—the great-grandfather of the present-day Kṛṣṇa consciousness movement. He was the spiritual master of Śrīla Gaurakiśora dāsa Bābājī and father of Śrīla Bhaktisiddhānta Sarasvatī, who was the spiritual master of Śrīla Prabhupāda.

Brahmā—the first created living being and secondary creator of the material universe.

Brahmajyoti—the spiritual effulgence emanating from the transcendental body of Lord Kṛṣṇa and illuminating the spiritual world.

Brahman—(1) the individual soul; (2) the impersonal, all- pervasive aspect of the Supreme; (3) the Supreme Personality of Godhead; (4) the *mahat-tattva,* or total material substance.

Brāhmaṇa—a person wise in Vedic knowledge, fixed in goodness, and knowledgeable of Brahman, the Absolute Truth; a member of the first Vedic social order.

Brahma-saṁhitā—a very ancient Sanskrit scripture recording the prayers of Brahmā to the Supreme Lord, Govinda.

C

Caitanya Mahāprabhu (1486-1534)—the Supreme Lord appearing as His own greatest devotee to teach love of God, especially through the process of congregational chanting of His holy names.

Caitanya-caritāmrta—a biography of Śrī Caitanya Mahāprabhu composed in Bengali in the late sixteenth century by Śrīla Kṛṣṇadāsa Kavirāja.

Cāṇakya Paṇḍita—the prime minister of King Candragupta. His aphorisms are still famous throughout India.

D

Deity of the Lord—the authorized form of Kṛṣṇa worshiped in temples.

Dhīra—one who is undisturbed in all circumstances.

G

Goloka Vṛndāvana (Kṛṣṇaloka)—the highest spiritual planet. Lord Kṛṣṇa's personal abode.

Gopīs—Kṛṣṇa's cowherd girlfriends, who are His most surrendered and confidential devotees.

Gosvāmī—a controller of the mind and senses; the title of one in the renounced, or *sannyāsa,* order.

Gṛhastha—regulated householder life; the second order of Vedic spiritual life; one in that order.

H

Hiraṇyakaśipu—a powerful demon who tormented his son Prahlāda, a great devotee, and was slain by Lord Nṛsiṁhadeva.

J

Jīva (jīvātmā)—the living entity, who is an eternal individual soul, part and parcel of the Supreme Lord.

Jñānī—one who cultivates knowledge by empirical speculation.

K

Kapila—the incarnation of the Supreme Lord who appeared as the son of Kardama Muni and Devahūti and taught the Kṛṣṇa conscious Sāṅkhya philosophy.

Karma—(1) material action performed according to scriptural regulations; (2) action pertaining to the development of the material body; (3) any material action which will incur a subsequent reaction; (4) the material reaction one incurs due to fruitive activities.

Karmī—one engaged in *karma,* fruitive activity; a materialist.

Kṛpaṇa—a miserly man who wastes his life by not striving for spiritual realization.

Kṣatriya—a warrior or administrator; the second Vedic social order.

M

Mahābhārata—Vyāsadeva's epic history of greater India, which includes the events of the Kurukṣetra war and the narration of the

Bhagavad-gītā.

Mantra—a transcendental sound or Vedic hymn that can deliver the mind from illusion.

Māyā—the inferior, illusory energy of the Supreme Lord, which rules over this material creation; also, forgetfulness of one's relationship with Kṛṣṇa.

Māyāvāda—the impersonal philosophy propounding the unqualified oneness of God and the living entities and the nonreality of manifest nature.

Māyāvādī—an impersonalist philosopher who conceives of the Absolute as ultimately formless and the living entity as equal to God.

N

Nārāyaṇa, Lord—the Supreme Lord in His majestic, four-armed form. An expansion of Kṛṣṇa, He presides over the Vaikuṇṭha planets.

Nṛsiṁhadeva—the half-man, half-lion incarnation of the Supreme Lord, who protected Prahlāda and killed the demon Hiraṇyakaśipu.

P

Paṇḍita—a scholar.

Parīkṣit Mahārāja—the emperor of the world who heard *Śrīmad-Bhāgavatam* from Śukadeva Gosvāmī and thus attained perfection.

Prahlāda Mahārāja—a devotee persecuted by his demoniac father Hiraṇyakaśipu but protected and saved by the Lord in the form of Nṛsiṁhadeva.

Prasādam—the Lord's mercy; food or other items spiritualized by being first offered to the Supreme Lord.

Pratyakṣa—the materialistic process of trying to understand things by one's own direct experience.

Purāṇas—eighteen literary supplements to the *Vedas,* discussing such topics as the creation of the universe, incarnations of the Supreme Lord and demigods, and the history of dynasties of saintly kings.

Pūtanā—a witch who was sent by Kaṁsa to appear in the form of a beautiful woman to kill baby Kṛṣṇa, but who was instead killed by Him and granted liberation.

S

Sannyāsī—one in the *sannyāsa* (renounced) order.

Śrīmad-Bhāgavatam—the *Purāṇa,* or history, written by Śrīla Vyāsadeva specifically to give a deep understanding of Lord Kṛṣṇa, His devotees, and devotional service.

Śruti—knowledge via hearing; also, the original Vedic scriptures (the *Vedas* and *Upaniṣads*), given directly by the Supreme Lord.

Śūdra—a laborer; the fourth of the Vedic social orders.

Śukadeva Gosvāmī—the great devotee sage who spoke *Śrīmad-Bhāgavatam* to King Parīkṣit just prior to the king's death.

Svāmī—See: Gosvāmī.

V

Vaikuṇṭha (Vaikuṇṭhaloka)—the spiritual world, where there is no anxiety.

Vaiṣṇava—a devotee of Lord Viṣṇu, or Kṛṣṇa.

Vaiśya—a farmer or merchant; the third Vedic social order.

Varṇas—the four Vedic social-occupational divisions of society, distinguished by quality of work and situation in the modes of nature (*guṇas*). *See also*: *Brāhmaṇa; Kṣatriya; Vaiśya;* and *Śūdra*.

Vedānta-sūtra—the philosophical treatise written by Vyāsadeva, consisting of aphorisms that embody the essential meaning of the *Upaniṣads.*

Vedas—the four original revealed scriptures (*Rg, Sāma, Atharva, and Yajur.*

Vivasvān—the demigod in charge of the sun.

Vyāsadeva—the incarnation of Lord Kṛṣṇa who gave the *Vedas, Purāṇas, Vedānta-sūtra, and Mahābhārata* to mankind.

Y

Yamarāja—the demigod who punishes the sinful after death.

Yamunā River—a river that flows through Vṛndāvana, India, and plays a central role in Kṛṣṇa's pastimes.

Yoga—spiritual discipline undergone to link oneself with the Supreme.

Yogī—a transcendentalist striving for union with the Supreme.